Ray Gardner was born in 1947. He worked at Royal Dutch Shell for 40 years in London, The Hague, and Houston. He retired in 2005 and then studied for a science degree at The Open University.

In 2018, Ray was diagnosed with myasthenia gravis and prostate cancer. Following successful treatment, he joined the Patient/Carer Advisory Group and the Senior Adult Oncology Programme at the Royal Marsden as a patient advocate. He then became involved in advocacy at the Institute of Cancer Research. He has also participated in a cancer research trial.

Ray is married, with two daughters, a son-in-law and two grandchildren.

To all the selfless cancer researchers and advocates
who work so tirelessly to find cures for this terrible disease.

Raymond Gardner

PUBLIC PARTICIPATION INVOLVEMENT AND ENGAGEMENT IN CANCER RESEARCH

AUSTIN MACAULEY PUBLISHERS

LONDON * CAMBRIDGE * NEW YORK * SHARJAH

A CIP catalogue record for this title is available from the British Library.

ISBN 9781035878642 (Paperback)
ISBN 9781035878659 (Hardback)
ISBN 9781035878666 (ePub e-book)

www.austinmacauley.com

First Published 2025
Austin Macauley Publishers Ltd®
1 Canada Square
Canary Wharf
London
E14 5AA

My grateful thanks to Martin Lee, who has given me unrestricted access and permission to use so much of his knowledge and information on this subject, and for his invaluable support. His dedication to the cause of public participation involvement and engagement in cancer research has been my inspiration to write this book.

Table of Contents

If the only miracle we are looking for is the big one…then we will most likely miss the other miracles that are unfolding before our very eyes, each and every day.

Deacon Wayne Charlton
Chaplain, Rogel Cancer Centre

Foreword

Every day, hundreds if not thousands of patients and the public go the extra mile to help make research happen in the UK. Their contribution is many and varied. One of the most important ways in which they make a difference in what we do is by improving the quality of research and how it is designed, conducted and delivered.

Within the NIHR, such is the extent to which the public has become involved that research is increasingly becoming a joint venture between patients and the public, researchers, clinicians and health professionals. If we are to meet the health and social challenges of the future then these partners must be empowered, encouraged and supported to work even closer together...

No researcher or institution who applies to the NIHR for funding can expect to be successful without a plan for public involvement that lay reviewers have scrutinised...Public involvement plays a vital role in strengthening the effectiveness and efficiency of the NIHR's Clinical Research Networks in recruiting people for studies.

Simon Denegri: Chair of the Breaking Boundaries Review
National Director for Patients and the Public in Research
Chair, INVOLVE
Foreword to ***Going the extra mile:***
Improving the nation's health and well-being through public involvement in research

Preface

Cancer is the most common human disease in the world. It is in fact not one disease but a collection of related diseases that can occur almost anywhere in the body. There are more than 200 different types of cancer, with over 10 million people worldwide dying from it every year. Last year, around 400,000 people were diagnosed with cancer in the UK, over 1,000 every single day, with only half expected to survive their diagnosis for 10 years or more. There are currently over three million people living with cancer in the UK; I became one of those when I was diagnosed with prostate cancer in 2018.

I was in my GP's surgery discussing a serious illness that had just been diagnosed (myasthenia gravis) when my local GP recommended a prostate screening antigen (PSA) blood test because of my age (I was 70 at the time). The PSA was high and I was subsequently diagnosed with stage IIC prostate cancer: I was a cancer statistic. Cancer Research UK estimate that more than 30% of new cancer cases in the over 70s are only diagnosed after treatment for another, unrelated, illness—a comorbidity. I was in fact a cancer statistic on two counts.

Whilst being treated for my cancer, I was invited to participate in a prostate cancer research trial. I consented but I had no idea at the time what I had signed up for as, to be honest, I was still in a bit of a daze from the cancer diagnosis. Some 5% of cancer patients are signed up for cancer trials: It is not known how many fully understand what they sign up for when they agree to become a trial participant, despite the best efforts of the researchers and clinicians. I was a cancer statistic on three (or four) counts.

In 2018, I was invited to a presentation at the Institute of Cancer Research (ICR) in Sutton, Surrey about involvement in research trials at The Royal Marsden (RM) and the ICR. I signed up to be an advocate. It is not known if members of the public fully understand what they are signing up for when they commit to becoming involved in cancer research. Perhaps, like me, they just felt a sense of obligation or duty—cancer statistic number four (or five).

Plato said *I know that I knew practically nothing...*(Plato, Apology, section 22d). That was my thoughts too when I first started as a patient advocate. As I became more involved in cancer research, I realised that I actually knew even less about cancer research than the little that I thought I knew (if you know what I mean). My initial experience forced me to reconsider my approach to cancer research trials very quickly (I have since found that I am by no means alone in that regard—cancer statistic number five—or six)!

I now understand that involvement in cancer research by members of the public is an under-utilised, under-estimated, under-resourced and poorly understood activity. My experiences have given me some insight into perhaps why. Many patients, let alone the general public, are confused about the difference between participation, involvement and engagement in cancer research trials. Some are put off by the idea of being a 'human guinea pig', some feel intimidated by the scientific terminology and jargon or think the roles are only for the well-educated, whilst some minority groups refuse to become involved because of perceived tokenism. Some decline because they feel uncomfortable about the idea of speaking in public—and some do not even know that these roles exist.

I decided to gather as much information as I could about public participation, involvement and engagement—firstly to try to ensure that I was not wasting the researchers' time with inane or irrelevant questions, and secondly, so that I could focus my own thoughts into the right areas. I now know that there is an awful lot of literature on the subject (mostly found by using the various online search engines available), but I also discovered that this information is like having different pieces of a jigsaw puzzle scattered in different rooms. I couldn't find any one book on the subject that brought it all together...so I decided to write one.

This book aims to take the mystery out of public participation involvement and engagement in cancer research. Reading the book will hopefully encourage more and, equally importantly, more diverse patients and members of the public to find out exactly what participating, becoming involved or engaged in cancer research trials actually means. By unlocking this door to public participation, involvement and engagement, I hope to give the reader enough background information for them to be able to make an immediate, positive and lasting public contribution to cancer research.

If this book encourages just one person to enrol as a participant in a trial or to become an advocate, I shall consider the effort worthwhile and the book a success.

I hope you enjoy the book.

Introduction

Cancer can affect anyone—regardless of race, colour, national origin, sex, religion, age or social standing. If meaningful research into cancer is to be carried out it is therefore crucial that the recruitment of any group of trial participants, or advocates who are involved with researchers, reflects as closely as possible the profile of the people who are likely to suffer from that particular cancer. Recruiting enough participants for a cancer trial or enlisting advocates to collaborate with researchers on trial design and management is difficult for researchers; getting the right *profile* of recruits onto trials or into advocacy is an even bigger challenge.

Have you ever been asked if you would consider taking part in a cancer research trial or perhaps become involved? If you have then your first thoughts perhaps turn to thinking about the implications…is it safe? How much time will it take up? How much will it cost me for extra travel costs? What does participation or involvement or engagement actually mean and what is the difference? You might well have other questions too but couldn't seem to get your questions answered and didn't want to trouble very busy staff, or you don't have the time or energy or technology available to research your questions. The chances are that you would politely ask for time to think about it and then not bother to follow up, or just decline.

This book is intended to try to change that. It is not meant to be a teaching manual; it only scratches the surface of cancer and cancer research. Its sole purpose is to pull together enough information about public participation involvement and engagement in cancer research in one place to help inform the public about what it means, with the aim of giving them the encouragement to find out more, feel informed and confident enough to get involved, and to then make an immediate, positive and lasting contribution when they do.

Becoming familiar with the process and terminology is key to unlocking the door to the secrets of cancer research. Parts 1 and 2 therefore focus on the biology of the human body and how cancer develops, Part 3 then explains how cancer is diagnosed and treated. Part 4 examines how cancer research trials work and Part 5 describes the roles of participation involvement and engagement in those trials. There is also a comprehensive glossary at the end of the book that explains some of the more common medical words, jargon and acronyms used in cancer research; it will be useful reference material should you decide to go ahead and become a trial participant or an advocate.

One final point: there are many terms used to describe patient and public participation involvement and engagement in medical research. I have opted to use the following National Institute for Health and Care Research (NIHR) definitions throughout this book[i]:

Public: includes patients, potential patients, carers and people who use health and social care services, as well as people from organisations that represent people who use those services (Whilst all of us are current, former or potential users of health and social care services, there is an important distinction to be made between the perspectives of the public and the perspectives of people who have a professional role in health and social care services).

Participation: where people take part in a research study.

Involvement: where members of the public are actively involved in research projects and research organisations.

Engagement: where information and knowledge about research is provided and disseminated.

When referenced in this book, the term PPIE will therefore mean Public Participation, Involvement and Engagement as defined above.

Part I
The Human Body

Biology and Terminology

The smallest unit of life is the cell.
So, if your cells are healthy, you are healthy.

Mike Murphy—Professor of Mitochondrial Redox Biology
Cambridge University

1: Introduction

You will, of course, have a general understanding of how the human body works, but it may be helpful to you to have a basic understanding of the biology of the human body to better comprehend how and why cancer develops, and how it is diagnosed and treated if you are considering becoming a trial participant or involved in trial development or oversight.

A 'human' is any living or extinct member of the family '*homo sapiens*', characterised by superior intelligence, articulate speech, and erect carriage. About 99% of the mass of a human body is made up of the molecules of six chemical elements: oxygen, carbon, hydrogen, nitrogen, calcium, and phosphorus. Most of the remaining 1% is composed of another five elements: potassium, sulphur, sodium, chlorine, and magnesium. In total the average human body contains traces of 61 of the 94 naturally occurring chemical elements, but only half of them play an active role in sustaining life. Over 50% of the human body is water. The human body is a highly developed single structure and is arguably the most complex organism on the planet. It is a single structure that contains trillions of molecules that combine to form microscopic elements that work together to sustain its life. These are called cells.

Cells are the basic building blocks of humans. Cells need nutrients and oxygen to live and then they expel the resultant unwanted waste—with many of these cells living deep inside the human body and not in direct contact with the outside world. Most cells in large multicellular organisms do not directly exchange substances like nutrients and wastes with the *external* environment, instead, they are surrounded by an *internal* environment of extracellular fluid— literally, fluid outside of cells. The cells get oxygen and nutrients from this extracellular fluid and release waste products into it. Humans have specialised systems that maintain their internal environment, keeping it stable and able to provide for the needs of the cells[ii].

Cells combine together to form tissues that, in turn, form organs which then integrate into organ systems. Together, cells, tissues, organs, and organ systems form this multicellular organism we call the human body. This highly complex arrangement is necessary to ensure that the cells deep inside the human body get the food to survive and to ensure that all waste products are expelled.

2: Cells

DNA

Cells provide structure to the human body, absorb nutrients from food, convert those nutrients into energy, and carry out other specialised functions. Cells are the body's hereditary material and replicate themselves during cell regeneration. It is estimated that there are approximately 37 trillion human cells in the average adult body and every cell is pretty unique[iii]. Inside each human cell is the nucleus (centre). The nucleus is a cell's control centre, directing cells to grow, mature, divide, or die.

The nucleus is home to 23 pairs of chromosomes, which contain everyone's individual deoxyribonucleic acid (DNA) sequence. The information contained in our DNA is necessary for us to develop, survive and reproduce. Each DNA sequence contains specific instructions describing how to make a protein known as a gene. The collection of genes within the DNA is called the genome. A genome is the whole of a DNA strand, a complex double-helix-shaped molecule, unique to you as an individual. Each genome contains all the information needed to build and maintain that particular organism throughout its life. Your genome is the total content of your own DNA; it contains instructions that helped you develop from a single cell into what you are today.

Each molecule of DNA is a double helix, and the building blocks of a DNA double helix are base pairs. Each base pair is attached to a sugar and a phosphate molecule which together are called a nucleotide. Nucleotides are arranged in two long strands to form the double-helix spiral. Base pairs contribute to this folded structure. The DNA double-helix molecule is formed from two complementary strands of nucleotides held together by hydrogen bonds between guanine-cytosine, and adenine-thymine, the so-called G-C and A-T 'base pairs' (figure 1).

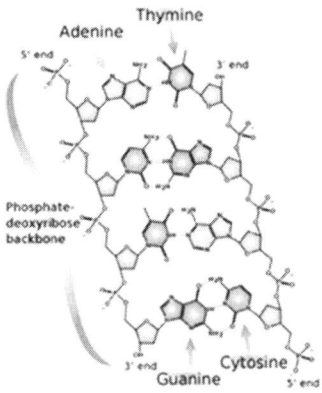

Figure 1: A schematic view of a DNA double-helix structure. Two single DNA strands comprised of the sugar-phosphate backbone and the alternating bases are linked together. (Source: Linko, Veikko. (2011). DNA-Based Applications in Molecular Electronics. Accessed on 8 February 2024)

If a double helix is unwound to a flat plan the resultant structure is like a ladder, with the base pairs forming the ladder's rungs and the sugar and phosphate molecules forming the vertical sides of the ladder (figure 2). In reality, the flat structure is twisted into the double helix on the right.

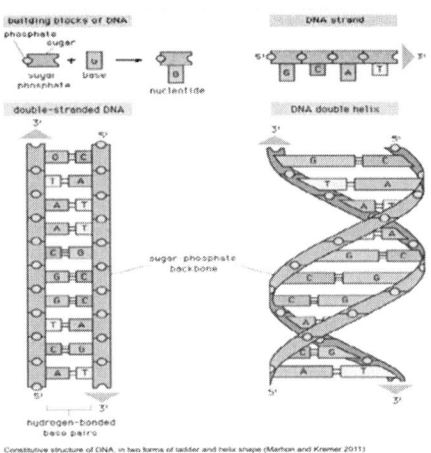

Figure 2: Simplified DNA in a flat plane
https://www.researchgate.net/figure/Constitutive-structure-of-DNA-in-two-forms-of-ladder-and-helix-shape-Marhon-and-Kremer_fig1_341944099 (Accessed on 14 January 2024)

Each DNA strand is used by the body as a template. The DNA strand is clever, having the ability to repair itself when damaged, help organs to function, and to control growth and development. Each strand of DNA in the double helix serves as a pattern for duplicating the sequence of base pairs. This is critical when cells divide because each new cell must have an exact copy of the DNA present in the old cell for it to survive.

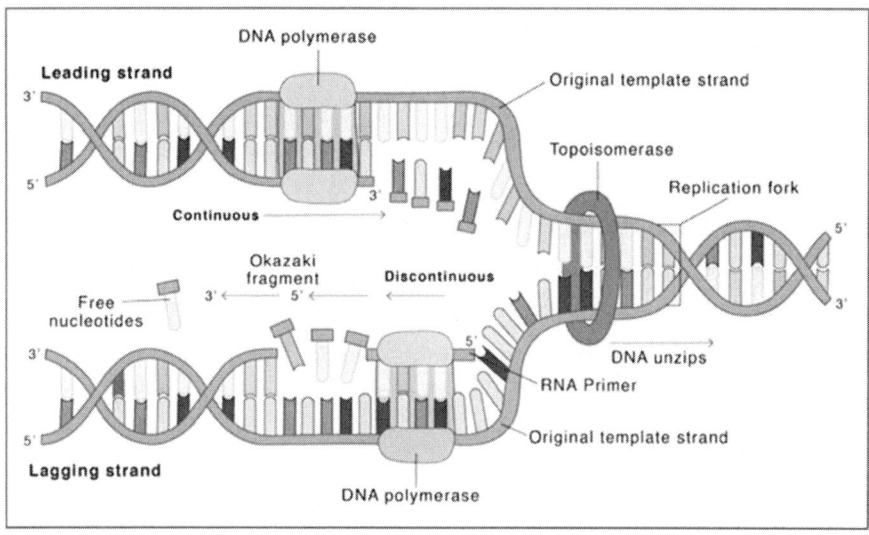

Figure 3: DNA replication (https://www.sciencefacts.net/dna-replication.html)
(Accessed on 14 January 2024)

The order of the base pairs in your DNA is your unique code and controls the function of your DNA. Your DNA is you!

The DNA of any two people is 99.9% identical, it is the differences in the remaining 0.1% that hold important clues about the causes of cancer in the damaged cells. DNA repair genes are involved in fixing damaged DNA. Cells with mutations in these genes tend to develop additional mutations in other genes and changes in their chromosomes, such as duplications and deletions of chromosome parts. Together, these mutations can cause the cells to become cancerous[iv].

CELL TYPES

There are a number of important cell types in cancer research and treatment:

STEM CELLS

Stem cells provide new cells for the body as it grows and replace specialised cells that are damaged or lost. They have two unique properties; they can divide over and over again to produce new cells and, when they divide, they can also change into the other types of cells that make up the human body. Both red and white blood cells originate from stem cells.

T-CELLS

T-cells are a subtype of white blood cells; they play a key role in fighting cancer. T-cells are part of the body's 'cell-mediated' immunity, the part of the immune system which directly kills bacteria, viruses, and cancer cells[v]. They are part of what is known as the cancer-immunity cycle. As cancer cells die, they release antigens—substances that can be recognised by the immune system. Antigens from the cancer cells are taken up on the cell surface of special immune cells called antigen-presenting cells (APCs) so that other immune cells can identify the antigens of interest. In the lymph nodes, the APCs activate the T-cells and teach them to recognise the tumour cells. The T-cells travel via the blood vessels to reach the tumour, infiltrate it, recognise the cancer cells and kill them. There are several types of T-cells:

- **Cytotoxic** T-cells find and directly attack foreign bodies in the body such as bacteria, viruses, and cancer cells.
- **Helper** T-cells recruit other immune cells and organise an immune response.
- **Regulatory** T-cells are believed to suppress the immune system so that it does not overreact (as it does in autoimmune diseases).
- **Natural killer** T-cells are cytotoxic T-cells that need to be pre-activated and differentiated to do their work. Natural killer cells and natural killer T-cells are subsets of lymphocytes that share common ground. Both can rapidly respond to the presence of tumour cells and participate in anti-tumour immune responses.
- **Memory** T-cells remember markers on the surface of bacteria, viruses, or cancer cells that they have seen before and react accordingly.

The T-cell is a 'chimeric antigen receptor' (CAR). T-cell therapy is a promising new way to get T-cells to fight cancer by changing them under laboratory conditions so they can find and destroy cancer cells (they can also be called CAR T-cells). T-cells are the major participants in anti-tumour immunity because more T-cells are present in the vicinity of tumour tissues than B-cells.

B-CELLS

B-cells create a type of protein called an antibody which binds to pathogens, or to foreign substances such as cancers, to neutralise them. B-cells can inhibit tumour development through the production of these tumour-reactive antibodies, promoting tumour killing by the NK cells.

Tissue structures are made up of a huge number of like cells and are more complicated than single cells.

3: Tissues Organs And Organ Systems

TISSUES

The many types of cells in the human body are organised into four broad categories of tissue: epithelial, connective, muscle, and nervous:

- **Connective** tissue supports other tissues and binds them together (bone, blood, and lymph tissues).
- **Epithelial** tissue provides a covering (skin) for the linings of the various passages inside the body.
- **Muscle** tissue includes muscles such as striated (voluntary) muscles that move the skeleton, or smooth muscles such as those surrounding the stomach.
- **Nerve** tissue is the body's internal communication system, carrying electro-chemical signalling in the form of nerve impulses round the body. It is made up of nerve cells called neurons.

Different tissues are made up of different types of cells depending on their purpose and function within the body. Each of these categories is characterised by specific functions that contribute to the overall health and maintenance of the body. Two or more types of tissue organised together to serve a particular function are called organs.

ORGANS

Organs such as the heart, the lungs, the stomach, the kidneys, the skin, and the liver, are organised to serve a particular function. For example, the heart pumps blood, the lungs bring in oxygen and eliminate carbon dioxide, and the skin provides a barrier to protect internal structures from the external environment. Most organs contain all four tissue types.

At each level of organisation, the body has evolved to optimise the functionality of that particular structure. Not surprisingly, therefore, the cells in the small intestine that absorb nutrients look different to the muscle cells needed for body movement.

The skin is very different, providing a barrier to protect internal structures from the external environment. Skin tissue is made up of multiple layers of tissue with different cells that act together. The skin is the largest organ in the body.

Organs are grouped into organ systems which work together to carry out a particular function in the body.

ORGANS SYSTEMS

There are 12 major organ systems in the body: circulatory (cardiovascular), digestive, endocrine, immune, integumentary, lymphatic, muscular, nervous, reproductive, respiratory, skeletal, and urinary. Each organ system has a very specific function in the human body:

- **Cardiovascular**: Consists of the heart, arteries, veins, and capillaries. They work together to provide blood flow to all parts of the body, carrying oxygen, nutrients, and hormones to cells, and remove waste products, such as carbon dioxide, away from the cells by circulating blood.
- **Digestive**: Processes foods and absorbs nutrients, minerals, vitamins, and water.
- **Endocrine**: Provides communication within the body via hormones and directs long-term change in other organ systems to maintain stability within the body.
- **Immune**: Defends against microbial pathogens and other diseases.
- **Integumentary**: Provides protection from injury and fluid loss and provides physical defence against infection by microorganisms.
- **Muscular**: Provides movement, support, and heat production.
- **Lymphatic**: A network of organs, nodes, ducts and vessels that make and move lymph (a colourless fluid) from tissue to the bloodstream. The lymphatic system consists of capillaries, tubes, vessels and glands that carry lymph around the body. It is a crucial part of the body's immune

31

system. Lymph vessels are present in all parts of the body just like arteries and veins in the blood system. Lymph is rich in white blood cells which fight and destroy damaged and abnormal cells, including cancer cells.

- **Nervous**: Collects, transfers, and processes information and directs short-term change in other organ systems.
- **Reproductive**: Produces sex cells and hormones.
- **Respiratory**: Delivers air to sites where gas exchanges occur.
- **Skeletal**: Supports and protects soft tissues of the body; provides movement at joints; produces blood cells; and stores minerals.
- **Urinary**: Removes excess water, salts, and waste products from the blood and body.

Just as the organs within an organ system work to accomplish their task so the different organ systems also collaborate to keep the body running. For example, the respiratory system and the circulatory system work closely together to deliver oxygen to cells and get rid of the carbon dioxide the cells produce, the circulatory system picks up oxygen in the lungs and drops it off in the tissues, performing the reverse service for carbon dioxide. The lungs expel the carbon dioxide and bring in new oxygen-containing air. Only when both systems are working together can oxygen and carbon dioxide be exchanged between cells and the environment.

IMMUNE SYSTEM

There are two branches of the immune system, the 'innate' immune system and the 'adaptive' immune system[vi]:

- The innate immune system provides a general defence against common pathogens (any bacteria, virus, or other disease-causing microorganism), which is why it is also known as the nonspecific immune system, and
- the adaptive immune system, which targets specific threats and learns how to launch precise responses against viruses or bacteria with which the body has already come into contact.

The various components of the immune system work together to provide both types of protection. The cardiovascular and lymphatic systems are designed to protect us from illness and disease and are very important in preserving our well-being. The lymphatic system can be considered as the body's immune response system. It is a combination of what we have at birth (hereditary, or built-in, immunity) and what we develop during our lifetime as a defence response to contracting illness and diseases (acquired immunity). The lymphatic system normally helps to trap and destroy cancer cells as well as other pathogens. However, cancer cells can sometimes get trapped in lymph nodes close to the cancer and may then start to grow there.

Both the blood and lymphatics systems rely on a supply of white and red blood cells and blood platelets.

4: Summary

The human body system is a complex combination of trillions of microscopic cells capable of working together to serve a common purpose—growth, reproduction and survival. Each part of the system depends on the other parts to perform tasks that cannot be achieved by those single parts acting alone.

The survival of the human body depends on the integrated activity of all of its organ systems. A disruption of the structure is a sign of injury or disease. Such changes can be detected through histology, the microscopic study of tissue appearance, organisation, and function. If any or all of the parts do not carry out their specific task then the body will eventually die.

When cells grow old or become damaged, they die, and new cells take their place. Sometimes this orderly process breaks down, and abnormal or damaged cells grow and multiply when they shouldn't, and they don't die. It is these cells in our body that can be prone to deformity during reproduction.

This is cancer.

Part II
Cancer

Genes and Mutations

The discovery that viral genes cause cancer was made by Peyton Rous, a medical pathologist whose imagination was aroused when a chicken breeder brought him a hen with a tumour.

Joseph L Goldstein—Biochemist
Nobel Prize winner in Physiology or Medicine (1978)

1: Introduction

Cancer is the abnormal growth of cells that results in a mass known as a tumour. Cancer can start in almost any cell in the human body and is the most common human disease in the world. Cancer is caused by changes (mutations) to normal genes during DNA replication. Most of these mutations are automatically corrected but some are not. When the mutation lies within the genes that control cell growth then uncontrolled growth of the mutated cell can occur, which can lead to new and abnormal growth of tissue in the body—a neoplasm. A neoplasm is an abnormal growth of tissue that can be either benign (non-cancerous) or malignant (cancerous). Benign tumours (non-cancerous neoplasms) usually grow slowly but malignant tumours (cancerous neoplasms) can grow rapidly, depending upon the type of cancer, often forming a localised mass or lump. Many cancers form solid tumours but cancers of the blood, such as leukaemia, generally do not. A cancerous growth also has the potential to spread to other parts of the body to form new tumours (a process called metastasis).

Benign tumours do not spread into, nor invade, nearby tissues. When removed, benign tumours usually do not grow back, whereas cancerous tumours sometimes do. Benign tumours can sometimes be quite large however and thus can still cause serious symptoms or even be life-threatening, for example, benign tumours in the brain.

Understanding more about diseases caused by a single gene (using genetics) and complex diseases such as cancer, caused by multiple genes and environmental factors (using genomics) can lead to earlier diagnoses, interventions, and targeted treatments.

2: Gene Mutations

HALLMARKS OF CANCER

Each cell has a built-in growth control, which in normal circumstances defines the growth and multiplication behaviour of the cell. These two control mechanisms are called 'tumour suppressor genes' and 'proto-oncogenes'. In normal circumstances, these two genes work together; proto-oncogenes instruct the cells to grow or multiply, whereas tumour suppressor genes instruct the cell to stop multiplying. If the tumour suppressor gene or proto-oncogene are damaged, they cease to function properly and the cells can continue to multiply without stopping, eventually creating cancerous tumours. Although the generic term 'cancer' comprises a diverse group of diseases, one characteristic and unifying feature is the creation of abnormal cells that grow beyond these natural boundaries.

In 2000, Hanahan and Weinberg proposed six 'hallmarks of cancer'[vii] that together form the fundamental principle of this malignant transformation. They are:

- Cell growth and division without the appropriate signals
- Evasion of growth suppressors
- Continuous growth and division immortality
- Activating invasion and metastasis
- Promoting blood cell destruction
- Avoidance of programmed death cells

Normal cells respond to complex instructions of division, growth and death. Cancer cells do not: They divide more rapidly than normal cells, refuse to die, and have the ability to replace themselves at will, outside the framework of normally regimented cells. Cancer cells are therefore normal cells that have gone wrong and are beginning to live a life of their own.

They have mutated.

HEREDITARY AND ACQUIRED MUTATION

The genes we are born with (those that we inherit from our biological parents) may include hereditary (or germline) mutations, increasing the risk of certain cancers. For example, the breast cancer (BRCA) genes are part of a complex structure that repairs double-strand breaks in DNA. The most commonly affected genes in hereditary breast and ovarian cancer are the BRCA1 and BRCA2 genes. Around 3% of breast cancers and 10% of ovarian cancers result from inherited mutations in the BRCA1 and BRCA2 genes.

It typically takes more than one gene mutation for a cell to become a cancer cell but when someone has inherited an abnormal copy of a gene, their cells already start out with one mutation. This makes it easier (and quicker) for other mutations to happen, which can lead to a cell becoming a cancer cell. This is why cancers related to inherited mutations tend to occur earlier in life than cancers of the same type that are not inherited.

Acquired gene mutations are different; they are not inherited from a parent. Instead, they develop at some point during a person's life. Acquired mutations occur in one cell, and then are passed on to any new cells that come from that cell. This mutation cannot be passed on to a person's children because it does not affect their sperm or egg cells. This type of mutation is also called a sporadic mutation or a somatic mutation. Acquired mutations can happen for different reasons. Sometimes they happen when a cell's DNA is damaged, such as after being exposed to radiation or certain chemicals, but often these mutations occur randomly, without having an outside cause. For example, during the complex process when a cell divides to make two new cells, the cell must make another exact copy of all of its DNA, but sometimes mistakes (mutations) occur whilst this is happening. Every time a cell divides is another chance for gene mutations to occur. The number of mutations in our cells can build up over time, which is why we have a higher risk of cancer as we get older.

Acquired gene mutations are a much more common cause of cancer than inherited mutations.

3: Metastatic Cancer

METASTASIS

For a cancer to spread in the body, some primary cancer cells must break away from their primary site. Figure 4 illustrates a primary tumour that has grown (developed) enough to break through the basement membrane. This allows the cancerous cells to escape from the primary tumour and enter either the lymph or blood capillaries to gain access to other regions of the body through the lymphatic or blood system networks. These are known as free cancer cells. They will continue to circulate round the body looking for a new home until they can find somewhere that they can settle and grow.

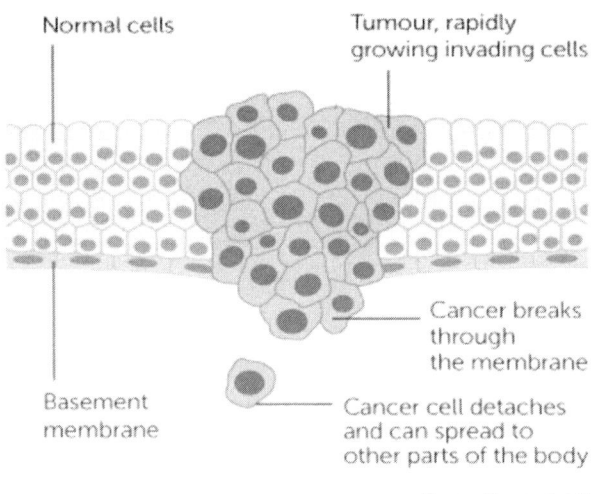

Figure 4: A cancer tumour breaking out of a primary site (CRUK
https://www.cancerresearchuk.org/about-cancer/what-is-cancer/how-cancer-can-spread Accessed 14 January 2024)

Using the lymph node or the blood networks as a mode of transport around the body, the cancer cell eventually becomes lodged in a capillary. Once the cancer has become attached, it grows and breaks into surrounding healthy tissue causing secondary cancer. The cells are from the original primary tumour so the secondary cancer is representative of the primary tumour.

The cancer has metastasised.

METASTATIC DEVELOPMENT

Once diagnosed, a cancer tumour is often referred to as the primary tumour. The spread of cancer cells from the primary tumour site to adjacent healthy tissue or distant body organs is known as metastasis or metastatic development. When cancer cells detach from the primary tumour site and spread to other parts of the body, this is called secondary or metastatic cancer. Metastatic cancer is most common in stage IV cancers, although it can happen earlier. The later the cancer stage, the harder it is to cure or manage and the lower the survival expectations.

There is often a misconception regarding what metastatic (secondary) cancer actually is. Secondary cancer is not cancer recurring at the original site after a period of remission, nor is it another cancer in a different part of the body, which is known as a multiple primary malignancy (MPM). For example, assume a patient has breast cancer, the primary tumour is therefore in the breast (obviously). The cancer then spreads (or metastasises) to the lungs, creating a secondary tumour in the lung. This secondary tumour in the lung is secondary breast cancer (or breast cancer with lung metastases); it is still breast cancer and is made up of metastatic breast cancer cells, not lung cancer cells. It is not lung cancer, as some would assume, even though the cancer has now spread to the lungs!

TUMOUR PROGRESSION

Cell mutations can accumulate over many years before the condition becomes cancerous, which also helps explain why a majority of cancers occur in older people.

In addition, some cancers are not obvious, which may explain why 30% of patients over 70 are only diagnosed with cancer after hospitalisation with another illness (a comorbidity).

4: Types Of Cancer

Doctors divide cancer into types based on where it begins, the four main types being:

- **Carcinoma** begins in the skin or the tissue that covers the surface of internal organs and glands. Carcinomas usually form solid tumours. They are the most common type of cancer, examples include prostate, breast, lung and colorectal cancer.
- **Sarcoma** begins in the tissues that support and connect the body. A sarcoma can develop in fat, muscles, nerves, tendons, joints, blood vessels, lymph vessels, cartilage, or bone.
- **Leukaemia** is a cancer of the blood. Leukaemia begins when healthy blood cells change and grow uncontrollably. The four main types of leukaemia are acute lymphocytic, chronic lymphatic, acute myeloid and chronic myeloid leukaemia.
- **Lymphoma** is a cancer that begins in the lymphatic system. The lymphatic system is a network of vessels and glands that help fight infection. There are two main types of lymphomas: Hodgkin lymphoma and non-Hodgkin lymphoma.

More than half of all cancers diagnoses are either breast, prostate, lung or bowel cancers with the 20 most common cancers making up over 93% of all known cancers.

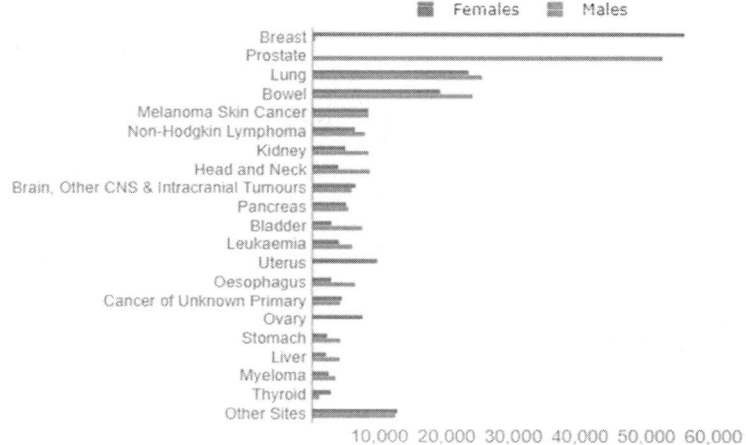

Table 1: The 20 Most Common Cancers 2016-2018
Source: https://www.cancerresearchuk.org/health-
professional/cancer-statistics-for-the-uk

(Data in this chart do not sum to all the cancers combined because 'Brain, other CNS (central nervous system) and intracranial' includes tumours that are malignant and non-malignant but only the malignant tumours are included in 'all cancers combined' total.) (Accessed on 2 February 2024)

5: Summary

Cancer is a genetic disease; it is created by a cell mutation that interferes with the normal cycle of healthy cells. It can, in principle, start in any cell in the body and it uses the body's own fluid transmission systems to spread as metastatic secondary cancer.

Statistics from both the American Cancer Society and the World Health Organisation suggest that one in two men and one in three women will be diagnosed with some form of cancer in their lifetime...but the risk of dying from cancer has decreased. Better screening, early diagnosis, more effective treatments, and the application of lifestyle changes have all contributed to reducing the risk of dying from cancer.

Cancer however is a disease of the ageing. More than half of all cancer diagnoses occur in patients aged 65 or older, with that number expected to increase to over two-thirds by 2040. This is not because the incidence of cancer is increasing but is more a testimony to the improved ability of health systems to cure non-cancer cases, which has led to many patients now living long enough for their mutated cancer cells to grow within their body to a point where they become the primary health issue.

There are more than 200 different types of cancer[viii], each being diagnosed and treated in a particular way.

Part III
Tests & Therapeutics

Diagnosis and Treatment

Cancer is a word, not a sentence.

John Diamond—Journalist

.

1: Introduction

Medicine is the science or practice of the diagnosis, treatment, and prevention of disease in the human body; it is the field of health and healing. Medicine includes nurses, doctors, and various specialists. It covers diagnosis, treatment, and prevention of disease, medical research, and many other aspects of health. Medicine aims to promote and maintain health and well-being.

The study of cancer is called oncology. The purpose of studying cancer is to develop safe and effective methods to prevent, detect, diagnose, treat, and, ultimately, cure the collection of diseases called cancer. An oncologist is a doctor who treats cancer and provides medical care for a person diagnosed with cancer. An oncologist may also be called a cancer specialist. The field of oncology has three major treatment areas[ix]:

- **Medical** oncologists treat cancer using medication such as chemotherapy, immunotherapy and targeted therapy.
- **Radiation** oncologists treat cancer using radiation therapy, which is the use of high-energy X-rays or other particles to destroy cancer cells.
- **Surgical** oncologists treat cancer using surgery including the removal of a tumour and nearby tissue during an operation. This type of surgeon can also perform certain types of biopsies to help diagnose cancer.

There are also medical terms for those oncologists who specialise in caring for specific groups of patients or groups of cancers. For example:

- **Geriatric** oncologists work with people with cancer who are aged 65 or over. Older adults can have additional challenges such as comorbidities. Geriatric oncologists specialise in providing the best care for older adults.

- **Gynaecological** oncologists treat cancers in such reproductive organs as the cervix, fallopian tubes, ovaries, uterus, vagina, and vulva.
- **Haematological** oncologists treat blood cancers, such as leukaemia, lymphoma, and myeloma.
- **Neuro**-oncologists treat cancers of the brain, spine, and nervous system.
- **Paediatric** oncologists treat cancer in children and young adults. Some types of cancer occur most often in these younger age groups.
- **Thoracic** oncologists treat cancers inside the chest area, including the lungs and oesophagus.
- **Urological** oncologists treat cancers in the genital-urinary systems, such as the bladder, kidneys, penis, prostate gland, and testicles.

An oncologist manages a patient's care throughout the course of the disease, starting with the diagnosis. An oncologist's role includes:

- recommending tests to determine whether a person has cancer,
- explaining a cancer diagnosis, including the type and stage of the cancer,
- talking about all treatment options and your treatment choice,
- delivering quality and compassionate care, and
- helping manage symptoms and side effects of cancer and its treatment.

A person's cancer treatment plan may include more than one type of treatment, such as surgery, cancer medications, and/or radiation therapy. That means different types of oncologists and other health care providers working together in a multidisciplinary team (MDT) to determine a patient's overall treatment…their systemic anti-cancer treatment (SACT) plan.

2: Prevention

RISK FACTORS

You have read that cancer is not a single disease but a group of related diseases. Many things, such as our genes, our lifestyle, and the environment around us can increase or decrease our risk of getting cancer.

Factors that are known to **increase** the risk of cancer include cigarette smoking and tobacco use, exposure to radiation (both ultraviolet radiation from sunlight and ionising radiation such as that used in tests to determine if cancer is present in the body), the use of immune-suppressive medicines after organ transplants, and certain viruses.

Factors that are known to **affect** the risk of cancer include (a poor) diet, being overweight, excessive alcohol consumption, lack of physical activity, diabetes and over-exposure to certain environmental risk factors.

ACTIONS

Cancer prevention is the action taken to reduce the risk of getting cancer. This can include maintaining a healthy lifestyle, avoiding exposure to known cancer-causing substances, and taking medicines or vaccines that can prevent cancer from developing. Scientists study the risk factors (anything that increases your chance of developing cancer) and protective factors (anything that decreases your chance of developing cancer) to find ways to prevent cancers from starting. Examples include:

- Establishing ways to avoid or control things known to cause cancer (e.g., cigarette smoking);
- Recommending (changes to) a diet (although it is not certain that this works) and lifestyle (alcohol is known to increase the risk of certain cancers);

- Developing and introducing tests to identify precancerous conditions early (precancerous conditions are conditions that may become cancer);
- Developing and introducing medicines to treat a precancerous condition or to keep cancer from starting using chemo-prevention (Two vaccines to prevent infection by cancer-causing agents have already been developed; one is a vaccine to prevent infection with Hepatitis B virus whilst the other protects against infection with the strains of human papillomavirus [HPV] that cause cervical cancer);
- Risk-reducing surgery (for example a prophylactic mastectomy can lower breast cancer risk by more than 90% in certain patients[x]);

Some risk factors for cancer can be avoided (for example, by stopping, or not starting, smoking) but many cannot be avoided (for example, inherited faulty genes).

3: Detection

Cancer is not one disease but a collection of related diseases that can occur almost anywhere in the body. At its most basic, cancer is a disease of the genes in the cells of the body. Detecting cancer that is in its early stages (either through screening or diagnosis) followed by effective treatment provides the best chance for a cure.

SYMPTOMS

Symptoms can affect specific areas of the body but signs can also be more general, including weight loss, tiredness (fatigue) or unexplained pain. Some possible signs of cancer, such as a lump, are better known than others but this does not mean that they are more important or more likely to be cancer.

The same cancer can also affect different people in different ways. The type of symptoms one person may have can be different to another, and some people may not even have any symptoms. However, if a GP believes that a patient is showing possible signs of cancer the patient will be referred to a cancer specialist for further tests.

DIAGNOSIS

If you have a symptom or a screening test result that suggests you might have cancer, your specialist will then try to find out whether it is actually cancer or some other cause. They may order laboratory tests, imaging tests (scans), or other tests or procedures. You may also need a biopsy, which is often the only way to be certain that you have cancer. Testing can be broadly split into three areas— laboratory tests, imaging and biopsies (although the doctor may also use interviews with the patient to get a feel for your family background and lifestyle).

LABORATORY TESTS AND RESULTS

It is possible to have a normal result for many tests even if you have cancer (a false negative), and conversely, it is also possible to have test results that are outside the normal range of that test even if you are healthy (a false positive). Laboratory tests alone cannot say for sure if you have cancer or any other disease, for example, a high prostate screening antigen (PSA) result may be indicative of prostate cancer or a false positive, and so the next step is usually some form of imaging to see if a tumour can be identified.

IMAGING

Image tests create pictures of areas inside the body that may help the doctor see whether a tumour is present and how large it is. Imaging tests are one of the following:

- **Computed (Axial) Tomography** (C(A)T): Scans use an x-ray machine linked to a computer to take a series of pictures of a body's organs from different angles. These pictures are used to create detailed 3-D images of the inside of the body.
- **Magnetic Resonance Imaging** (MRI): Machines use a powerful magnet and radio wave to take pictures of the body in 'slices'. These slices are combined to create a detailed image of the inside of the body, showing places where there may be tumours.
- **Ultrasound**: Examinations use high-energy sound waves that people cannot hear. The sound waves echo off tissues inside the body. A computer uses these echoes to create pictures of areas inside the body. This picture is called a sonogram.
- **X-ray**: Uses low doses of radiation to create pictures inside the body and can show changes caused by cancer or other medical conditions

NUCLEAR MEDICINE

Nuclear medicine is a very specific area of medical imaging. It provides information to aid clinicians in the diagnosis of cancer. Nuclear medicine can indicate exactly where the disease is located in the body, whether it is responding to treatment as planned, or if it has spread to secondary locations within the body. Nuclear medicine is used for disease discovery, diagnosis and treatment management, as well as establishing if any recurrence of the disease is evident during patient follow-up appointments. It is a medical specialty that uses radioactive tracers (radiopharmaceuticals) to assess bodily functions and to diagnose, manage and treat disease, and nuclear medicine imaging techniques as a diagnostic aid.

RADIOACTIVE TRACERS

Radioactive tracers (radiopharmaceuticals) are made up of carrier molecules that are bonded tightly to a radioactive atom. These carrier molecules vary greatly depending on the purpose of the scan. Some tracers employ molecules that interact with a specific protein or sugar in the body and can even utilise the patient's own cells. For most diagnostic studies in nuclear medicine, the radioactive tracer is administered to a patient by intravenous injection. However, a radioactive tracer may also be administered by inhalation, oral ingestion, or direct injection into an organ. The mode of tracer administration will depend on the disease that is to be investigated.

NUCLEAR MEDICINE IMAGING

Nuclear medicine imaging is an important diagnostic tool in clinical decision-making. Specially designed cameras allow clinicians to track the path of these radioactive tracers inside a patient's body:

- **Single-Photon Emission Computed Tomogr**aphy (SPECT) scans use radioactive material to take pictures of the inside of the body (This type of scan may also be called a radionuclide scan). Before the scan a small amount of radioactive material is injected into the bloodstream (sometimes called a tracer). This radioactive material flows through the bloodstream and collects in certain bones or organs before decaying and exiting the body.
- **Positron Emission Tomography** (PET) scans are another specific type of nuclear scan. Because cancer cells often take up more glucose than healthy cells, PET scans can make detailed 3-D pictures of areas inside the body where glucose is taken up.

- **Bone Scans** check for abnormal areas of, or damage in, the bones. They may be used to diagnose bone cancer or to find out whether cancer has spread to the bones from elsewhere (metastatic bone tumours).

SPECT and PET scans are the two most common imaging modalities in nuclear medicine.

USING IMAGING MODALITIES

Each of the common imaging modalities has differing patient benefits and is selected by the referring clinician to provide the information needed to assist either in disease diagnosis or to determine the selection of a treatment pathway. This selection process can be broadly divided into two categories; those that define very precisely anatomical detail and those that produce functional or molecular images.

The first method, using computed tomography (CT) and magnetic resonance imaging (MRI) scans, provides minute details on lesion location, size, morphology and structural changes to surrounding tissue, but will only deliver limited information as to how the tumour is functioning.

The second method, using PET and SPECT scans, can give a detailed insight into the tumour physiology down to the molecular level but cannot provide the anatomical detail needed.

However, combining these methods (either PET/CT, PET/MRI or SPECT/CT) enables the integration of both the anatomical and functional aspects into a single approach. The introduction of this 'hybrid' scanning technique for imaging has enabled the characteristics of tumours in all stages of development to be identified.

The hybrid image generated from (for example) a PET/CT scan is actually two images captured of the patient during a single scan intervention, overlaid on a single image. This image is then interpreted by the radiologist and passed to the patient's clinician who will use the information to determine the patient's status and recommend a treatment pathway.

BIOPSIES

In most cases, doctors will also need to do a biopsy to be absolutely certain that cancer is present. A biopsy is a procedure in which the doctor removes a sample of suspected abnormal tissue. A liquid biopsy is a test carried out on a sample of blood to look for cancer cells or pieces of DNA from tumour cells that are sometimes released into the blood, whereas tumour markers measure substances that are produced by cancer cells or other cells of the body in response to cancer.

Most tumour markers are made by both normal cells and cancer cells but the markers are produced at much higher levels by cancer cells. A pathologist looks at the tissue under a microscope and runs other tests on the cells in the sample. The pathologist describes the findings in a pathology report, which contains details about the diagnosis. The information in the pathology reports also helps show what treatment options might work.

STAGING

Staging is a method used by cancer doctors to describe the size of a cancer and how far it has grown. When doctors first diagnose cancer, they carry out tests to check how big the cancer is, whether it has spread into surrounding tissues or if it has spread to other parts of the body. There are two main types of cancer staging systems. The first is the TNM system, which was developed by the American Joint Committee on Cancer. Doctors use the results from diagnostic tests and scans to answer the following questions:

- Tumour (T): How large is the primary tumour and where is it located?
- Node (N): Has the tumour spread to the lymph nodes? If so, where and how many?
- Metastasis (M): Has the cancer spread? If so, where and how much?

The results are combined to determine the stage of cancer for each person. There are five stages: stage 0 (zero) and stages I through IV (1 through 4). Each stage provides a common way of describing the cancer so doctors can work together to plan the best treatments. If the biopsy and other tests show that cancer is present, more tests might be required to help the doctor plan the right treatment.

The second is the number system. Number staging systems use the TNM system to further divide cancers into stages. Most types of cancer have four stages, numbered from 1 to 4 (or I to IV):

- **Stage 1** usually means the cancer is small and contained within the organ it started in.

- **Stage 2** usually means that the tumour is larger than in Stage 1 but the cancer hasn't spread into surrounding tissues, although it may have spread into lymph nodes close to the tumour.
- **Stage 3** usually means the cancer is larger. It may have started to spread into surrounding tissues and there are cancer cells in nearby lymph nodes.
- **Stage 4** means the cancer has spread from where it started to another body organ. This is secondary or metastatic cancer.
- Sometimes doctors use the letters A, B or C to further divide the number categories. For example, Stage 2C prostate cancer.

CARCINOMA IN SITU

Carcinoma in situ is sometimes called stage 0 cancer or an 'in situ neoplasm'. This means that there is a group of abnormal cells in one area of the body and the cells may develop into cancer at some point in the future. The change in these cells is called dysplasia. The number of abnormal cells is too small to form a tumour.

For some cancers, other pathology studies are also carried out to find out the grade of the tumour, or tumour markers are studied to find out the risk group that the cancer falls into. All of this information is important for deciding on the best treatment. The tumour may also be tested further for other tumour markers or biomarkers. Once the cancer has been located, staged and graded discussions on treatment options can commence.

4: Treatment

TYPES

There are many types of cancer treatment; the type of treatment that you receive will depend on the type of cancer you have and how advanced it is. If the cancer is in just one place doctors may recommend a local treatment such as surgery or radiotherapy, but most people have a combination of treatments, such as surgery with chemotherapy and radiation therapy; these are called systemic anti-cancer treatments (SACTs). SACTs include cellular targeted therapies, chemotherapy, hormone therapy, and immunotherapy. Before any treatment begins a specialist would also discuss wider issues such as implications for quality of life post any recommended treatment. Cancer treatment options include:

SURGERY

Surgery is a procedure by which cancer is surgically removed from the body. Surgery is a common first-line treatment for many types of cancers. It is one of many treatment options and will be dependent on the type of cancer, the size of the tumour, where it is in the body, if the tumour is safely accessible, whether it has spread into a secondary metastatic cancer to other parts of the body, the general health of the patient, and if the patient can tolerate the impact of the anaesthetic and surgery. During surgery, the tumour is removed together with a portion of surrounding healthy cells to ensure as much as possible that all active cancer cells have been removed. If a patient presents with multiple cancer sites due to secondary metastatic cancer, surgery may not be a viable treatment pathway and so other options would need to be considered.

CHEMOTHERAPY

Chemotherapy uses powerful drugs that are targeted to destroy, shrink, or control fast-growing cancer cells. Chemotherapy can be used:

- Before surgery or radiotherapy to shrink cancer tumours to a more manageable size (neoadjuvant chemotherapy);
- After cancer surgery or radiotherapy to destroy any remaining cancer cells (adjuvant chemotherapy).
- As a stand-alone curative cancer treatment, for example, to treat cancers of the blood or lymphatic system such as leukaemia and lymphoma;
- To treat cancer recurrence, or for cancer that has spread to other parts of the body (metastatic cancer);
- To relieve symptoms where a cure is not possible (palliative chemotherapy);
- Combined with radiotherapy to increase the efficacy of radiotherapy treatment (chemoradiation).

Chemotherapy is normally administered in cycles. This helps allow the body to recover before repeating the chemotherapy treatment. The treatment and rest period is the treatment cycle. Several of these treatment cycles make up a course of chemotherapy.

There are more than 100 different types of chemotherapy drugs available, and chemotherapy is delivered either by intravenous means or tablets. However, chemotherapy is cytotoxic, meaning it can damage normal, healthy cells in addition to cancer cells and can also have side effects (although these can wear off after treatment stops).

RADIOTHERAPY

External beam radiation therapy, otherwise known simply as radiotherapy, is considered the most effective cancer treatment after surgery. It uses high doses of radiation to kill cancer cells and shrink tumours. Radiotherapy can be used as a curative treatment, to improve the effect of other treatments, be combined with chemotherapy (chemoradiation) or before surgery (neo-adjuvant radiotherapy).

It is also used after surgery or chemotherapy treatments to neutralise any missed cancer cells to reduce the risk of recurrence of cancer and to relieve symptoms (palliative radiotherapy).

Radiotherapy is a targeted procedure but the radiation beam cannot distinguish between cancer and healthy tissue, therefore patient movement must be kept to a minimum to limit damage to healthy surrounding tissue whilst maximising the impact on the cancer cells present.

The types of radiotherapy are:

- **Conformal Radiotherapy**; radiotherapy beams are shaped to fit the target area.
- **Intensity-Modulated Radiotherapy** (IMRT) shapes the radiotherapy beam, thus allowing different intensities of the dose to different parts of the target area, preserving healthy tissue surrounding the tumour.
- **Volumetric Modulated Arc Radiotherapy** (VMAT) is a modified IMRT system, where the machine rotates around the patient whilst reshaping the beam during treatment, thus providing more accurate treatment in a faster time.
- **Image Guided Radiotherapy** (IGRT) utilises scans taken before the treatment to allow radiographers to adjust the treatment area before and during each treatment to give a very accurate treatment.
- **4D Radiotherapy** (4DRT) uses special radiotherapy machines that can take images of the tumour during treatment. This allows adjustment of the radiotherapy during treatment.
- **Stereotactic Radiotherapy** uses multiple beams of radiation to the target, allowing high doses of radiotherapy to be given to very small areas of the body, making the process very accurate and also reducing side effects.
- **Total Body Irradiation** (TBI) delivers a single large dose of radiation to the whole body, and although not in common use it is used on some stem cell transplant patients.
- **Proton Beam Therapy** uses proton radiation rather than X-Rays to destroy cancer cells. Whereas X-Rays penetrate right through the body, proton beams can be stopped at the target area.
- **Internal Beam Radiotherapy** delivers a high dose of radiation directly to the tumour. This involves implanting radioactive materials at the site

of the cancer tumour. Internal radiotherapy delivers a high dose of radiation with fewer side effects than external beam radiotherapy. It delivers radiation from inside the body, close to the cancer, affecting less healthy cells. However, internal radiotherapy is only really suitable for smaller cancers.

- **Brachytherapy** is a type of internal beam radiotherapy. It involves radioactive implants in the form of seeds, ribbons, or wires. These are put into the body by insertion in or near the site of the cancer tumour or taken orally by the patient as a drink.

- **Radioactive Liquid Therapy** is an oral radioactive compound that the patient drinks.

- **Intraoperative Radiotherapy** is a single dose of radiotherapy which is administered during cancer surgery in the operating theatre.

Whichever type of radiation is used, the principle is the same—radiotherapy works by damaging the DNA in the cancer cells to prevent them from dividing and growing.

IMMUNOTHERAPY

Immunotherapy (also known as immune-oncology) uses the patient's own body's immune system to fight cancer. Immunotherapy is a type of biological therapy and can be used to fight a number of different cancers. By design, it can find and destroy infection, disease and faulty cells generated in the body, such as cancer cells. However, whilst the immune system can identify cancer cells, it may not in all cases be strong enough to kill them. Cancer cells have their own defence mechanism and can produce signals that prevent the immune system from attacking them, and cancer cells can both hide from and escape from the immune system. Cancer immunotherapy comes in a variety of forms, which include targeted antibodies, cancer vaccines, adoptive cell transfer, tumour-infecting viruses, checkpoint inhibitors, cytokines, and adjuvants.

Immunotherapies are a form of biotherapy (also called biologic therapy or biological response modifier [BRM] therapy) because they use materials from living organisms to fight disease. Some immunotherapy treatments use genetic engineering to enhance the body's immune cells' cancer-fighting capabilities and are commonly referred to as gene therapies. Many immunotherapy treatments for preventing, managing, or treating different cancers can also be used in combination with surgery, chemotherapy, radiation, or targeted therapies to improve their effectiveness. Immunotherapy stimulates the patient's own immune system to recognise cancer cells as foreign bodies and kill those cancer cells.

There are a number of immune therapy treatments, each working in different ways to assist the immune system in recognising and attacking cancer cells. One example is CAR T-cell therapy, which involves collecting T-cells from the body and engineering them from T-cells to CAR T-cells under laboratory conditions. Once modified, the cells are returned to the blood stream. These CAR T-cells then have the ability to recognise and attack the cancer cells.

TARGETED THERAPY

Targeted therapy focuses on the changes in cancer cells that help them grow, divide and spread. Targeted therapy is usually in the form of tablet medication and is designed to attack cancer cells by targeting specific genes and proteins that are involved in the growth and survival of cancer cells.

Targeted drugs often work by blocking cancer cells from copying themselves. This means they can help stop a cancer cell from dividing and making new cancer cells. Targeted therapy is seen as a cornerstone of precision medicine.

PRECISION MEDICINE

Precision medicine is a form of treatment that uses specific information about an individual's genes and proteins to prevent, diagnose, and treat cancer. It is an approach that allows doctors to select and design treatments that are most likely to help patients based on a specific genetic understanding of their cancer. Precision medicine can offer tremendous opportunities to shape the future of healthcare. Currently, precision medicine is the most advanced in cancer. Precision medicine (or personalised medicine) has the potential to shift treatment from a reactive response to a proactive response, as the long-term ambition of precision medicine is that the treatment will be specifically tailored to the genetic changes in each person's specific cancer.

STEM CELL TRANSPLANTS

Stem cells are specialist cells which are produced by the bone marrow (a spongy tissue found in the centre of some bones) that can turn into any type of cell in the body. Stem cell transplants are procedures that restore blood-forming stem cells in cancer patients who have had their stem cells compromised or destroyed by high doses of cancer treatment such as chemotherapy or radiation therapy.

A stem cell transplant uses stem cells from a patient's, or a donor's, bloodstream. Blood-forming stem cells are important because they grow into different types of blood cells. Stem cells can become either red blood cells, carrying oxygen around the body, white blood cells, which help fight infection and disease, or platelets (which in turn help to control or stop bleeding). A stem cell transplant works on the principle of the destruction of unhealthy blood cells, replacing them with healthy stem cells removed from the blood or bone marrow of a suitable donor or the patient.

HORMONE THERAPY

Hormone therapy is used to treat cancers that use hormones to grow. Hormone therapy is considered a systemic therapy (it travels around the body) whereas surgery and radiation therapy are considered local treatments as they tend to focus on one specific area.

Hormone therapy uses medicines to block or lower the number of hormones in the body to slow down or stop the growth of cancer. Hormones are natural substances that are made by glands in the body. These hormones are carried around the body by the bloodstream and act as messengers between one part of our body and another. Hormones are responsible for many functions in our body, including the growth and activity of certain cells and organs.

Cancers that are hormone-sensitive include breast cancer, prostate cancer, ovarian cancer and womb cancer. Hormone therapy falls into two groups, broadly, those that block the body's ability to produce hormones and those that interfere with how hormones behave in the body. When used with other treatments, hormone therapy can make a cancer tumour smaller before surgery or radiation therapy. Hormone therapy can be administered in different ways including orally with tablets, by injection, or in some cases by surgery to remove a hormone-producing organ such as the prostate gland.

HYPERTHERMIA TREATMENT

Hyperthermia treatment is a cancer treatment where body tissue is exposed to high temperatures (up to 45°C) but with little or no harm to normal tissue. It does this by killing cancer cells and damaging proteins and other structures inside the cells. Variants include:

- **High-intensity Focused Ultrasound** (HIFU) is a type of local external hyperthermia treatment. HIFU uses ultrasound waves to create intense heat which destroys the cancer cells. MRI is generally used to guide the ultrasound beam.
- **Regional Hyperthermia** uses slightly lower heat levels to treat cancer tumours. The temperatures used in regional hyperthermia are usually between 40°C and 45°C. Regional hyperthermia may be used to heat large areas of tissue, such as an organ or limb.
- **Magnetic Nanoparticles Hyperthermia** treatment is a new technique for targeted therapeutic heating of cancer tumours. Magnetic nanoparticle hyperthermia is being studied as an adjuvant to conventional chemotherapy and radiotherapy.

RADIOFREQUENCY ABLATION

Radiofrequency ablation (RFA) uses electrical waves to raise the temperature of cancer cells to destroy them. A thin probe delivers an electrical current directly into the tumour using ultrasound, MRI or a CT scan to accurately guide the probe to the tumour. The probe delivers heat between 50°C and 100°C. This method is used to treat tumours that cannot be removed by surgery or in people who are not able to have surgery.

MICROWAVE ABLATION

Microwave ablation uses a much higher frequency range than RFA, generating higher temperature levels so it can treat a larger area of cancer. Similar to RFA, one or more probes deliver microwaves into the tumour.

LASER THERAPY

Laser therapy uses high-intensity focused light beams to treat cancer. Lasers can be used to either shrink or destroy cancer tumours or precancerous growths. Lasers are commonly used to treat superficial cancers on the surface of the body or the lining of internal organs. Lasers can also be used to relieve certain symptoms of cancer. Laser therapy can be used alone but is often combined with other treatments, such as surgery, chemotherapy or radiation therapy. In addition, lasers can seal nerve endings to reduce pain after surgery and seal lymph vessels to reduce swelling and limit the spread of tumour cells. Lasers are more accurate than standard surgical procedures, and so do less damage to the normal healthy tissues surrounding the cancer.

CRYOTHERAPY

Cryotherapy destroys cancer cells by freezing them with liquid nitrogen or argon gas. Cryotherapy is classed as a local cancer treatment; it does not treat any cancer cells in other parts of the body. A thin needle called a cryoprobe is used to deliver the liquid nitrogen or argon gas to the cancer tumour using image-guidance techniques. Cryotherapy is an alternative cancer treatment where surgical removal of a tumour may be difficult or, for some patients, impossible, but its long-term effectiveness is still being examined.

PHOTODYNAMIC THERAPY

A targeted drug is activated by light to kill cancer and other abnormal cells.

TREATMENT SIDE EFFECTS

Cancer treatments can cause side effects. Side effects are problems that occur when treatment affects healthy tissues or organs. Side effects vary from person to person, regardless of the type of cancer treatment being administered, even amongst people with the same type of cancer receiving the same treatment.

BLOOD CELLS AND PLATELETS

White blood cells are part of the immune system and the level of white cells can be reduced by cancer treatment. The white cells that fight infections are called neutrophils. When the number of white cells in the blood is low, infections are more likely. This is because there are fewer neutrophils to fight off bacteria and viruses. Treatments such as chemotherapy or radiotherapy can detrimentally affect white blood cell levels and the immune system by destroying white blood cells, leaving already weakened cancer patients at greater risk of illness or infection.

Red blood cells contain haemoglobin which carries oxygen around the body. Some cancer treatments can affect the level of haemoglobin in your blood. If the red blood cell count is low it is called anaemia and can increase tiredness. Some cancer treatments can make a patient anaemic. Breathlessness can occur if the amount of oxygen being carried around the body is reduced.

As well as red and white blood cells, there are platelets in the blood. Platelets help clot the blood to prevent bleeding. Certain cancers such as leukaemia or lymphoma can lower the platelet count, thus reducing the ability for blood to clot.

Cancer, and cancer treatment, can therefore affect the blood and so, during treatment, patients should expect regular blood tests to check the number of cells in the blood.

HOLISTIC APPROACH

Other factors considered when various cancer treatments are under consideration include not only the best patient outcome for the immediate cancer diagnosis but also the long-term quality of life for the patient post-treatment. Clinicians consider all circumstances surrounding a patient, including the patient's own wishes, and not just the cancer as a single component. The final choice of treatment will have balanced the cancer treatment against the long-term patient outcome and thus will not only look for the most beneficial treatment to increase patient survivability but also consider the best ongoing quality of life for the patient post-treatment.

TREATMENT RECORD

A treatment summary is completed by the clinician after a significant phase of a patient's cancer treatment. It describes the agreed treatment, potential side effects, and symptoms and signs of recurrence that the patient should monitor. It is designed to be shared with the person living with cancer, their family and support group, and their GP. The treatment summary aims to inform the GP and other primary care professionals of actions that need to be taken and who to contact with any questions or concerns. The cancer patient also receives a copy to improve their understanding and to be aware of anything to look out for during their recovery. The treatment summary can also be shared with other health professionals and used by the patient to evidence the patient's treatment, for example when arranging travel insurance. It will show everything a patient diagnosed with cancer needs to know about their treatment pathway.

REMISSION AND CURE

Whether someone's cancer can be cured depends on the type and stage of cancer, the type of treatment available to them, and other factors such as general health and age at the time of diagnosis and, ultimately, decisions taken by the patient regarding their quality of life preferences. Some cancers are more likely to be cured than others. But each cancer needs to be treated differently.

There isn't one cure for cancer.

A cure means that the cancer has gone away with treatment, no more treatment is needed, and the cancer is not expected to come back. However, it is rare that a doctor can be sure that cancer will never come back. In most cases, it takes time to know if the cancer might come back but the longer a person is cancer-free, the better the chance that the cancer will not return. More often than not, when treatment appears to be successful, doctors will say the cancer is 'in remission' rather than 'cured'.

Remission is the period of time when the cancer is responding to treatment or is under control. Often people think that remission means the cancer has been cured, but that may not be the case. For example, in 'complete remission,' all signs and symptoms of cancer go away and cancer cells cannot be found by any tests, whereas in 'partial remission,' the cancer shrinks but has not completely gone away.

Remissions can last anywhere from weeks to years. Treatment may or may not continue during remission, depending on the type of cancer. Complete remissions may go on for years and over time, your cancer may be thought to be cured. If cancer returns (recurrence), another remission may still be possible with further treatment.

5: Summary

You have now read about cancer, its origins in cells, the way in which cancer cells migrate through the body, and its potential to metastasise. Identification of the cancer and treatment options have also been discussed, but, it is a big 'but', there has been no reduction in new cases of cancer[xi]. Indeed, cancer cases are expected to continue to increase, because of better treatments for non-cancer causes of death. By far, the biggest risk factor for most cancers is now simply getting older. More than three-quarters of all people diagnosed with cancer in the UK are 60 and over[xii] because cancer is a disease of our genes. As we get older, deformities in our genes can accumulate, and it is these deformities that can provide the platform for cancerous cells to grow. The longer our lifespan, the greater the chance that these deformities build up, and thus the greater the risk of cancer developing.

No figures are yet available to determine if lifestyle changes will reduce the chances of cancer in years to come and research is ongoing into cancer prevention. However, preventing cancer is probably a limited option in the short term. That leaves research into cancer treatment and cure as the major focus. The purpose of research into cancer is to develop safe and effective methods to prevent, detect, diagnose, treat, and, ultimately, cure the collection of diseases called cancer.

Whatever cancer research, be it prevention, care or cure, the approach to cancer trials is the same.

Part Iv: Cancer Research

Trials and Tribulations
The Germ of an Idea

I would picture myself as a virus, or as a cancer cell, for example, and try to sense what it would be like to be either. I would also imagine myself as the immune system and I would try to reconstruct what I would do as an immune system engaged in combating a virus or cancer cell. When I had played through a series of such scenarios on a particular problem and had gained new insights, I would design laboratory experiments accordingly...

Jonas Salk—American physician and microbiologist

1: Introduction

Historical cancer research has helped to accumulate today's extensive knowledge about the biological processes involved in cancer's onset, its growth, how it spreads in the human body, and, most importantly, how it reacts to cancer treatments. The discoveries, through both success and failure, have led to the effective and targeted treatment and prevention strategies in use today. Breakthroughs in prevention, earlier detection, screening, diagnosis, and treatment have required partnerships and collaborations involving researchers, clinicians, patients, the public, and funders.

Clinicians and researchers often witness impressive treatment results during clinical practice or basic laboratory testing and may wish to pursue research to formally explore their ideas and experiences. Successful cancer research transforms and saves lives but, by its very nature, it is not an exact science. Progress is not always linear either but can be cyclical or ongoing. The research cycle flows from a clinician's or researcher's observations at the patient's bedside and back to the lab. Insights from one discipline influence others, and discoveries made in one cancer can sometimes offer new ideas to others. Tomorrow's advances will be the result of building on yesterday's discoveries and today's observations and ideas.

An obvious first step for anyone considering research into a particular area is to connect with experienced researchers to discuss their ideas for a study who may well ask, *What exactly is your research question?* Crystalising the germ of an idea into focused research is only the beginning. Not all ideas become research studies, and not all research studies are successful. Even if they are then that germ of an idea can still take 10 to 15 years for a drug or treatment pathway to go through all the phases of a clinical trial[xiii] and become standard of care.

2: Process

GOAL

The goal of research is to develop knowledge that improves human health or increases the understanding of human biology. Research can be divided into four broad categories:

- **Basic Research**: Basic research is the study of animals, cells, molecules, or genes to gain new knowledge about cellular and molecular changes that occur naturally or during the development of a disease. Basic research is also referred to as laboratory research or preclinical research.
- **Translational Research**: Translational research seeks to accelerate the application of discoveries in the laboratory to clinical practice. This is often described by researchers as moving advances in research from 'bench to bedside'.
- **Population Research**: Population research (also known as epidemiological research) is the study of causes and patterns of occurrence of cancer and evaluation of risk. Epidemiologists study the patterns, causes, and effects of health and diseases in defined groups. Population research is highly collaborative and can span the spectrum from basic to clinical research.
- **Clinical Research**: Clinical research involves clinical trials that study a particular patient or group of patients, including their behaviours, or use materials from humans, such as blood or tissue samples, to learn about a disease, how the healthy body works, or how it responds to treatment.

CLINICAL TRIALS

The first step to finding out if a new drug or treatment pathway is safe and effective is to test it on patients in clinical research trials. Clinical trials are a key part of cancer research and are at the heart of all medical advances in cancer treatment. Clinical trials look at new ways to prevent, detect, or treat a disease. They are medical research studies that generally involve patients as participants. Researchers initially test possible new drugs in a laboratory. If the results look promising, they are thoroughly and carefully tested in cancer patients. Clinical cancer trials can look at:

- Risks and causes: how genetics, lifestyle and other factors increase the risk of cancer
- Prevention: using drugs or lifestyle changes to reduce risk
- Screening: tests for people with a higher than average risk of cancer or for everyone
- Diagnosis: new tests, scans or procedures
- Treatments: new dosages of existing or new drugs or combinations of drugs, or new ways or types of treatment
- Controlling symptoms or side effects: new drugs or complementary therapies

The goal of clinical research trials is to determine if these treatment, prevention, and behaviour approaches are safe and effective. The benefits of furthering new knowledge both within the profession and in the wider healthcare system are both clear and compelling. This necessitates the involvement of clinicians, researchers, patients and the public to collaborate in forming a research question, plan the research, execute the research, interpret the results, and move successful research findings into practice. The shared effort between clinicians, researchers, patients and the public increases the likelihood that research initiatives will then be relevant to practice.

There are two main types of trials or studies—interventional and observational[xiv]:

- Interventional trials aim to find out more about a particular intervention, or treatment. A computer allocates trial participants taking part into different treatment groups so that the research team can compare the results.

- Observational studies aim to find out what happens to people in different situations. The research team observe the participants taking part but does not influence what treatments people have. The participants taking part are not put into treatment groups.

Clinical trials to test new cancer treatments involve a series of steps, called phases, that must follow strict guidelines.

PHASES

A new treatment will go through several phases before it can be accepted into clinical practice, with each phase having a different purpose. Most of the time when you take part in a clinical trial, you will only be in one phase of a study. Treatments move through the phases, but patients do not. Early clinical trial phases (phases 0, 1 and 2) test for safety, such as what the side effects are and to determine what a safe dose is. Later phases (phases 3 and 4) compare the treatment to the current standard of care.

- **Phase 0:** These studies determine if a drug behaves in the way that researchers expect after their laboratory analysis. Phase 0 studies usually only involve a very small number of patients and a very small dose of a drug. The dose of the drug is too small to treat the cancer, but side effects are less likely. Phase 0 studies aim to find out if the drug reaches the cancer cells, how cancer cells in the body react to the drug (if the drug reaches it) and what happens to the drug in the rest of the body.
- **Phase 1 (I)**: In a phase 1 clinical trial, researchers determine whether a new treatment is safe, what its potential side effects might be, whether patients can tolerate it, the highest dose that patients can tolerate, and if the treatment affects the cancer. These trials are carried out on a small group of patients (around 15 to 30). They are often 'dose-escalation' studies where the first few patients receive a very small dose of the drug. The dosage is increased in the next few patients if all goes well and so on until the most effective dose level is determined. All the time, the researchers monitor the patients for any side effects.

- **Phase 2 (II)**: Phase 2 clinical trials include more patients (50 to 100) to see if the new treatment seems to work against the cancer, such as by shrinking tumours or slowing the growth. Sometimes in a phase 2 trial, a new drug or therapy is compared with another treatment already in use, or with a dummy drug (a placebo). Researchers also want to see how the new treatment affects the body and how it fights cancer. Researchers continue to study drug tolerance and any side effects.

- **Phase 3 (III)**: In a phase 3 clinical trial, researchers compare the treatment to the current standard of care (best practice) to compare which works better. They also compare the side effects of the two treatments. Patients are randomly assigned to one of the treatments to ensure that any differences are real and not the result of differences in the people in each group. Phase 3 trials include large numbers of patients (from 100 to several thousand) to ensure that the results are valid.

- **Phase 4 (IV)**: Phase 4 clinical trials look at long-term safety and effectiveness that take place after a new treatment has been approved and the drug or treatment is available to the general public. These trials are done after a drug has been shown to work and has been licensed. Treatment effectiveness and safety are monitored in large, diverse populations. More information is gathered as more and more patients use the drug or device over a longer period of time. Phase 4 clinical trials are rarely conducted.

RANDOMISATION

Trial participants will be allocated to one of the trial groups at random. This process is called 'randomisation' and is usually done by a computer. Some phase 2 trials and most phase 3 trials are randomised. Often there is one group who has the standard treatment they would have if they were not in the trial (but without knowing). Cancer Research UK has published a useful table summarising the phases of a cancer research trial (See table 2).

Phase	Number taking part	Types of cancer being treated	Main aims of the trial	Randomised?
0	5-15	Often lots of cancer types	Testing a low dose to see if it is harmful or not	No
1	15-30	Often lots of cancer types	Trying to find the optimal dose of treatment, if there are any side effects and what happens to the body during treatment	No
2	50-100	Usually, one or two specific cancer types, sometimes more	Trying to find the optimal dose of treatment, finding out more about side effects and if, and how well, the treatment works	Sometimes
3	100 +	Usually, one specific cancer type, sometimes more	Comparing the new treatment with the current standard of care or to a dummy drug	Usually
4	varies	Usually, one specific cancer type, sometimes more	Finding out more about the long-term benefits and side effects	No

Table 2: Trial Phases At A Glance (adapted from Cancer Research UK table) (Accessed on 14 January 2024)

Most trials are just one phase but some trials can cover more than one phase, so trials may then be written as a phase 1/2 trial or a phase 2/3 trial. Results from phase 1, 2 and 3 trials are used to make policy decisions about approving new treatments, or existing treatments for new conditions.

Before any new medicine can be used to treat people in the UK, it has to go through a strictly monitored development process. After passing the clinical trials, a licence must be granted before it can be made available for wider use. Licences are only granted if strict safety and quality standards are met. In the UK, licences are granted by the Medicines and Healthcare Products Regulatory Agency (MHRA).

Whatever the trial phase or protocol, researchers will have to secure some form of funding.

3: Funding

The positive outcomes of cancer research trials that have looked into the prevention, diagnosis and treatment of cancer have helped save millions of lives, but any research trial is expensive to run due to the cost of:

- Medical treatments, procedures and tests,
- Research staff needed to run the trial and collect the data,
- Analytical and computer technology staff to analyse the results,
- Administrative staff to handle paperwork, protocol oversight, data collection and results production and dissemination, and
- Extra tests, travel costs and hospital stays for trial participants.

Funding for cancer research comes from three main sources, public funding, charities and 'big pharma'—the global pharmaceutical industry.

PUBLIC FUNDING

The National Health Service (NHS) was born out of a long-held ideal that good healthcare should be available to all, regardless of wealth. Primarily funded by the UK Government from general taxation, the UK's healthcare and health research (including cancer research) is now overseen by the Department of Health and Social Care (DHSC). There are various bodies that publicly fund health research in the UK spearheaded by the National Institute for Health Research (NIHR).

NATIONAL INSTITUTE FOR HEALTH RESEARCH

The NIHR is the research arm of the NHS. It was created in April 2006[xv] under the government's health research strategy to 'create a health research system in which the NHS supports outstanding individuals, working in world-class facilities, conducting leading-edge research focused on the needs of patients and the public.' Since then the NIHR has become widely recognised for transforming the health research landscape in the NHS by creating collaborative relationships between universities and the NHS, enhancing the clinical workforce (by reversing the decline in clinical academic numbers), reducing the time between the translation of scientific breakthroughs into bedside benefits for patients, and equally importantly, as an exemplar for public and patient involvement. The NIHR is a major funder of health research within the UK, including cancer research projects.

NIHR BIOMEDICAL RESEARCH CENTRES

Biomedical Research Centres (BRCs) are partnerships between world-class research universities and NHS organisations to bring together academics and clinicians to translate lab-based scientific breakthroughs into potential new patient treatments, diagnostics and medical technologies. The BRCs receive funding to create an environment where experimental medicine can thrive. They attract the best scientists and contribute to both the local and national economy. BRC funding supports researchers in the development of innovative research ideas that can then go on to attract investment from other funders, furthering the nation's economic growth. The centres undertake research across a range of disease and therapeutic areas, such as genomics, stem cell therapy, cancer and regenerative medicine.

The NIHR awarded nearly £800 million to 20 Biomedical Research Centres across England, to 'translate scientific discoveries into new treatments, diagnostic tests and medical technologies to improve patients' lives'[xvi] in October 2022.

NIHR CLINICAL RESEARCH FACILITIES

The NIHR planned to invest a total of £112 million between 2017 and 2022 in Clinical Research Facilities (CRFs) in NHS hospitals where researchers deliver early-phase research[xvii]. The NIHR's 22 CRFs are purpose-built facilities in NHS hospitals where researchers deliver early-phase and complex studies. These facilities have dedicated spaces for high-risk experimental medicine studies, such as 'first-in-patient' trials and intensive later-phase studies. The facilities have cutting-edge clinical facilities, technologies and expertise and are designed to support high-intensity studies and overnight stays. NIHR CRFs are supported by the UKCRF Network, which provides best-practice guidance and tools to ensure each CRF delivers clinical trials to the highest standard. Researchers funded by the NIHR, the life sciences industry or other organisations can access assistance from skilled CRF clinical trial support staff, from study design, data collection and study management.

NIHR CLINICAL RESEARCH NETWORK

The NIHR Clinical Research Network (CRN) supported 1,287 studies on cancer (406 of which were new studies) and recruited nearly 100,000 patients as participants in the studies[xviii]. From April 2024, the CRN will transition to a new organisation, the NIHR Research Delivery Network (RDN)[xix].

NIHR EXPERIMENTAL CANCER MEDICINE CENTRES

Experimental Cancer Medicine Centres (ECMCs), located throughout England, act as an efficient and effective network for delivering pioneering, early-phase cancer trials, bringing together world-leading laboratory and clinical researchers to test new treatments for adults and children with cancer. The network of centres speeds up the process of cancer drug development, and the search for biomarkers, to diagnose cancer, predict the aggressiveness of the disease, or show whether a drug will be effective. The centres increase the capacity, safety and speed of early-phase cancer research in England, improving the success rates in developing new treatments for patients and ensuring that the UK remains at the forefront of international efforts to develop and test new treatments for cancer. The centres are associated with universities that have cancer research capabilities and are linked to local NHS hospitals. The NIHR funds 14 ECMCs across England in close partnership with Cancer Research UK.

NIHR INVENTION FOR INNOVATION

The cancer research landscape is not only about drugs; there is also a large investment in medical devices and equipment research. Invention for Innovation[xx] (i4i) is also sponsored by the NIHR. It is a research funding scheme essentially aimed at medical devices, in vitro (test tube) experiments, diagnostic devices and high-impact patient-focused digital health technologies plus the much-anticipated introduction of artificial intelligence (AI) into patient diagnosis, treatment and care. The aim of i4i is to develop technologies for everyday use in the NHS to provide more accurate cancer diagnosis and treatment pathways.

NIHR RESEARCH SUPPORT SERVICE

The Research Support Service (RSS) provides free and confidential advice to develop funding applications within the remit of the NIHR, including clinical, applied health and social care research, and post-award advice to award holders. RSS advisers have a wealth of experience and proven track records in supporting high-quality funding applications, supporting applications—not only to NIHR research programmes but also to other open, national, peer-reviewed funding competitions for applied health or social care research, including cancer charities.

CHARITABLE ORGANISATIONS

In the mid-nineteenth century, cancer was seen as an incurable disease, steeped in fear and denial but, perhaps surprisingly, it was also when the concept of public involvement in cancer research first started, mainly through fund-raising for research.

THE ROYAL MARSDEN HOSPITAL

The Royal Marsden Hospital (RMH) was the first hospital in the world dedicated to the study and treatment of cancer. It was founded in 1851 as the Free Cancer Hospital by Dr William Marsden, following the death of his wife from cancer, to classify tumours, research the causes, and find new treatments. The Institute of Cancer Research (ICR) was founded in 1909 as the Cancer Hospital Research Institute (CHRI) as a small research laboratory within what would become the RMH in Chelsea.

AMERICAN CANCER SOCIETY

The American Society for the Control of Cancer (ASCC) was co-founded by ten physicians and five lay people in 1913 to change the public's view of cancer, with donations focused on care. In 1945 the ASCC was reorganised as the American Cancer Society (ACS); it was the beginning of a new era for the organisation. In 1946, philanthropist Mary Lasker and her colleagues helped to raise more than $4 million for the Society—$1 million of which was used to establish and fund the ACS's ground-breaking research program.

LEUKAEMIA AND LYMPHOMA SOCIETY

The foundation of the Leukaemia and Lymphoma Society in 1949 in the USA by Rudolph and Antoinette de Villiers after the death of their son Robert from leukaemia is another early example. The organisation sponsored annual international research competitions with monetary awards to conduct research for treating leukaemia.

BLOOD CANCER UK

Blood Cancer UK was originally set up in 1960 as the Leukaemia Research Fund. The charity was started by the Eastwood family from Middlesbrough who began raising money following the death of their 6-year-old daughter Susan. Since its foundation Blood Cancer UK has invested over £500 million in a number of different research projects which have helped improve understanding, diagnosis and treatment of blood cancers.

CHILDREN'S CANCER AND LEUKAEMIA GROUP

Founded in 1977, the UK Children's Cancer Study Group (UKCCSG), the forerunner to the Children's Cancer and Leukaemia Group (CCLG), was formed to establish clinical trials in childhood cancer, to collect data and to offer an important clinical forum to advance knowledge into children's cancers.

THE BRITTA DOLAN MEMORIAL CANCER FUND

In 1987, Patrick Dolan set up The Britta Dolan Memorial Cancer Fund after his wife, Britta Dolan, died from bowel cancer. Patrick was frustrated with the lack of treatment options and support for bowel cancer patients in the UK, which meant he had to turn to specialists in America. With the support of colleagues and friends, Patrick raised half a million pounds and obtained financial support for a doctor and research nurse to undertake clinical trials in the UK.

BLADDER CANCER ADVOCACY NETWORK

The Bladder Cancer Advocacy Network (BCAN) was founded in 2005 and is the only national advocacy organisation devoted to advancing bladder cancer research and supporting those impacted by the disease. The mission of BCAN is to increase public awareness about bladder cancer, advance bladder cancer research, and provide educational and support services.

CHARITY FUNDING TODAY

Over half of the funding stream for cancer research in the UK now originates from public donations to charitable organisations. There are (at the time of writing) at least 313 charitable organisations in the UK listed as donating to cancer research[xxi], the largest being Cancer Research UK (CRUK). CRUK is the largest independent cancer research organisation outside of the USA. In 2022-23, Cancer Research UK committed £398m towards cancer research[xxii]. CRUK receives no government funding for their research.

PHARMACEUTICAL COMPANIES

'Big Pharma' is a term used to refer to the global pharmaceutical industry. Big Pharma makes billions of dollars in profit every year through the research, development and patenting of effective drugs. In 2022, the pharmaceutical industry spent a massive US$ 200 billion worldwide on research and development covering all health research themes. To the pharmaceutical industry, cancer research is seriously big business, but it is not without its pitfalls. For example, in 2017, the most expensive new cancer tablet was Celgene's Idhifa (approved to treat a subset of leukaemia patients) with a treatment cost of $298,465 per person per year. Celgene was later acquired by Bristol Myers, which said in 2020 that a subsequent study of Idhifa failed to show that it had improved survival when compared to standard care[xxiii].

Within the United Kingdom, global pharmaceutical companies fund a large portion of cancer research. These pharmaceutical companies can run their own drug trials looking at drugs under in-house development. If a drug company is running a trial at a specific hospital, it pays the hospital for the costs of tests and costs associated with trial patients' hospital stays. The major pharmaceutical companies in the UK currently are GSK (GlaxoSmithKline), Johnson & Johnson, Pfizer, AstraZeneca, and Bayer.

SYNOPSIS

Cancer drugs are extremely costly but can generate high revenues, with costs of cancer treatment averaging around £17,000 per patient in the year of diagnosis[xxiv]. Money successfully invested into cancer research results in the introduction of new medications for patients, which improves cancer treatment, patient outcomes and a reduction in patient treatment burdens, but it can also see an increase in the price of drugs—as pharmaceutical companies charge a premium for newly researched and released drugs.

Researchers in all areas of the research landscape are likely to have their research funded by a mixture of grants from various government agencies, institutions, charitable foundations, private companies and industrial and pharmaceutical companies.

Cancer Research UK has published a toolkit[xxv] for researchers on how to plan, deliver and evaluate patient involvement when applying for funding; such is its importance and complexity.

Once the research question has been finalised, the protocols written and sanctioned, and funding obtained, the trial can begin.

4: Trial Framework

GOVERNANCE AND ETHICS

You will no doubt be relieved to hear that clinical trials involving cancer research are a highly regulated activity. Clinical trials must follow strict guidelines before, during and after a trial. The Medicines and Healthcare Products Regulatory Agency (MHRA) is the regulatory authority responsible for clinical trial approvals, oversight, and inspections in the UK. The MHRA grants permission for clinical trials to be conducted in accordance with the Medicines for Human Use (Clinical Trials) Regulations 2004 (MHCTR) and the Medicines for Human Use (Clinical Trials) Amendment Regulations 2006 (MHCTR2006)[xxvi]. The MHRA is an executive agency within the Department for Health and Social Care (DHSC).

The Secretary of State for the DHSC is authorised to make clinical trials regulations and amend or supplement the law relating to human medicines, taking into consideration the safety of human medicines, the availability of human medicines, and the likelihood of the UK being seen as a favourable place to carry out research relating to human medicines, conduct clinical trials, or manufacture or supply human medicines.

PROCESS

The process is complicated so the NIHR has developed a 'Clinical Trials Toolkit Routemap' to help researchers understand the requirements of the MHCTR regulations (see Figure 5).

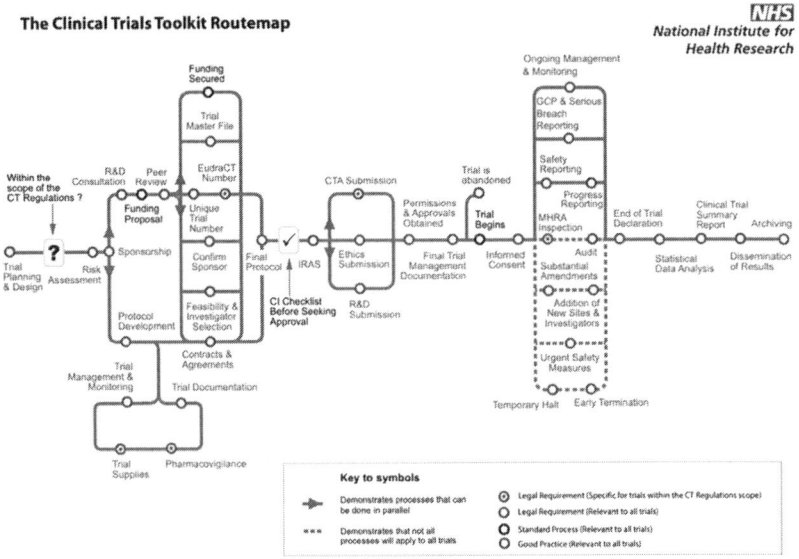

Figure 5: The Clinical Trials Toolkit Route map (NIHR https://www.ct-toolkit.ac.uk/routemap/)

INTEGRITY

The 'concordat to support research integrity[xxvii] asks universities, research institutes and individual researchers to commit to ensuring their work is underpinned by the highest standards of rigorous scrutiny and integrity. Indeed it can be very difficult for any research institution to get funding if they do not support this concordat.

APPROVAL AND OVERSIGHT

All clinical trials of medicines and studies on medical devices must be authorised by the MHRA. This is called Clinical Trial Authorisation (CTA). The process begins with the submission of the proposed trial protocol (the detailed plan of the trial) for a peer review.

PEER REVIEW

When researchers are considering asking for funding, a peer review will be required before funding is granted. A peer review can include doctors, other healthcare professionals and non-medical (lay) members of the public. The review will look at areas such as:

- the aim of the trial and how important the issue is,
- the design of the trial,
- whether people are likely to want to take part,
- the patient profile the research team are seeking,
- how the research team plans to analyse the results, and
- whether the research team have thought about all the possible issues.

ETHICS

The trial proposal is reviewed by a Research Ethics Committee (REC) which is generally organised by the Health Research Authority (HRA). Each committee has up to 15 members who are not involved with the trial in any way (they would have to declare a conflict of interest and withdraw if any involvement was identified). At least one in three of these people are members of the public who are not researchers or health professionals. RECs look after the rights, safety, dignity and well-being of those taking part in the trial. They assess each trial protocol against a set of standards, reviewing areas such as:

- whether the trial protocol has been peer-reviewed,
- the aim of the specific trial and how important the issue is for patients,
- how the research team plan to recruit trial participants,
- whether the likely benefits are greater than the possible risks,
- the qualifications and experience of the team running the trial,
- if the patient information sheet (PIS) is complete and easy to understand, and
- if extra information such as GP letters or patient questionnaires are well written.

Having reviewed the trial proposal the REC can ask the research team to make changes to, for example, the protocol or the patient information sheet, before they give the final go-ahead. Once satisfied the committee then determines if the trial is safe and ethical and can proceed. The researchers are then not allowed to change the protocol without telling the REC. The REC can stop the trial at any time if they have any concerns about the welfare of the participants taking part. At the end of the trial, the REC will get a copy of the results.

The REC will also maintain oversight of the trial. The research team must, for example, tell the REC if participants in the trial have had any unexpected side effects (adverse events). The ethics committee have the power to:

- stop the trial completely (i.e. earlier than planned),
- stop the trial temporarily to review the way forward,
- ask the research team to change the trial protocol because of adverse events, or
- simply to ask the research team to update the patient information sheet and informed consent form.

STOPPING TRIALS EARLY

Trials can be closed early if there is clear evidence that the trial treatment is obviously much better (or much worse) than the standard of care, or if people are having severe side effects from the treatment. However, researchers do not like closing trials early unless there is very strong evidence that one group of patients is doing much better than the other. Closing a trial early can make it difficult to interpret the results. For example, sometimes results may seem better for one treatment over another in the short term but this may not be the case in the long term.

A trial can also be closed early if patient recruitment is much slower than expected (for example the funder may decide that the trial is recruiting so slowly that it will take too long to come up with any meaningful results). It would not be a good use of funds to continue and, importantly, it is not ethical to continue entering patients into a trial that is not going to decide anything.

DATA MONITORING COMMITTEE

A data monitoring committee (DMC) is usually set up before a trial starts to look at the safety and design of the trial. The DMC will regularly check how the trial is proceeding at particular timepoints as set out in the protocol, monitoring:

- how many patients have withdrawn from the trial,
- if there have been any adverse side effects,

- patient feedback about benefits and side effects, and
- the results so far.
- At each time point, the DMC will review the progress to date and recommend that the trial either:
- continues as it is, or
- continues with some changes (such as increasing or changing the patient cohort), or
- stops early (for example because of adverse reactions), or
- runs for longer than originally planned.

If the data monitoring committee think there is a possibility the trial can prove something useful, but that more patient participants are needed to get enough results, they can suggest the trial runs for longer than planned (for example because a larger patient participation would be expected to give more representative results).

SITE APPROVAL

Any hospital that wishes to take part in a trial has to get approval from its NHS Research and Development (R&D) department, called a site-specific assessment (SSA). This assessment makes sure that the hospital has the staff, time, equipment and expertise to carry out the trial safely. The R&D department also looks at any other trials concurrently running at the hospital before giving permission as, for example, they may not have the capacity to run two trials recruiting similar patients. The trial team will then arrange training for the local hospital staff. This could be online or in person and should include anyone involved with the trial. This training includes doctors, research nurses, pharmacists and radiographers. Once everyone is familiar with the trial protocols and all the approvals are in place patient recruitment can start.

RESULTS
ANALYSIS

Once the 'end of trial' has been declared then statistical analysis of the results can begin. The primary target variable (the primary endpoint of the trial) should be the variable capable of providing the most clinically relevant and convincing evidence directly related to the primary objective of the trial. There should ideally be only one primary variable, usually an efficacy variable because the primary objective is generally to provide strong scientific evidence regarding the effectiveness of a specific drug or a treatment protocol. However, whilst drug safety and tolerability may not always be the primary variable it will always be an important consideration. Other possible primary variables include quality of life and health economics. Secondary variables are either supportive measurements related to the primary objective of the trial or measurements of effects related to any other secondary objectives.

Avoiding bias in clinical trials is crucial for the results to be interpreted correctly. The most important design techniques for avoiding bias are 'blinding' and 'randomisation,' and these should be normal features of most controlled clinical trials. Statistical analysis is a science and as such is a crucial element in the trial process. The European Medicines Agency has published a useful document 'Notes for Guidance on Statistical Principles for Clinical Trials'[xxviii] that explains statistical analysis.

DISSEMINATION

Once the results have been analysed and the conclusions reached then they can be shared with the scientific community (usually in the form of a detailed scientific paper) and the general public through (for example) a press release. In addition, it is important that surviving patient participants are also advised of the outcome of the trial (usually in the form of a lay summary). The European Commission has published a public health 'Good Lay Summary Practice Guide'[xxix] to help researchers write up research results in lay terms.

LONG-TERM RESULTS

Researchers can also continue to collect information about patients who have taken part in a trial long after they finish treatment, sometimes for years. This is partly to see how well the different treatments work in the long term and partly to find out about any possible long-term side effects.

PATIENT CONFIDENTIALITY AND DATA PROTECTION

Access to patient data is vital for research, but patient data must be stored safely and securely to ensure patient confidentiality. All research involving human participants, or data or samples derived from human participants (such as cohort studies or clinical trials) must include appropriate safeguards to protect the privacy of research participants.

5: Summary

Many people are only alive today because of successful cancer research. Cancer research trials are designed to test new ways to find, prevent, and treat cancer. They can also help doctors improve the quality of life for people with cancer by testing ways to manage the side effects of cancer and its treatment.

There are different types of cancer research trials, and each one could help researchers learn things that can help cancer sufferers in the future. Cancer trials require considerable funding due to the associated high costs of the trials and are subject to a rigorous control process, but the benefits of successful trials are high, both for patients' health and financially for the companies developing any successful new drugs.

Finding ways to prevent cancer, or to care for or cure it through earlier interventions or more effective treatments, is a fundamental research priority for the NHS if the projected long-term burden of cancer is to be reduced. Ensuring that cancer research is properly focused, and funding is effectively and efficiently spent, is the challenge for all.

All historical cancer trials have involved patient participation in some form. It is now widely accepted by the cancer research community that utilising and expanding upon the lived experience of anyone who has survived cancer[xxx], or someone who has supported a cancer sufferer, can significantly improve the way that research into cancer is conducted. Indeed, most cancer research funders now insist upon a clear demonstration of public advocacy even in initial funding applications.

Clinical trials need people of every age, health status, race, gender, ethnicity and cultural background to participate to ensure that the patient cohort on the trial is truly representative of the patient group that experiences that particular cancer. The same is true for advocacy, although experienced advocates can be used even if their cancer was of a different type to the one being studied.

Part V
Public Participation, Involvement And Engagement

To Boldly Go…Participation

The only way medical advancements can be made is if people volunteer to participate in clinical research. The research participant is just as necessary as the researcher in this partnership to advance health care.

Liz Martinez—Johns Hopkins Medicine Research Participant Advocate

Involvement

No matter how complicated the research or how brilliant the researcher, patients and the public always offer invaluable insights.

Dame Sally Davies—Chief Medical Officer (UK)

1: Introduction

The purpose of studying cancer is to develop safe and effective methods to prevent, detect, diagnose, treat, and ultimately cure the collections of diseases we call cancer. Successful cancer research will transform and save lives and, at the same time, reduce the economic burden that cancer has on everyone. The total cost of cancer in the UK was estimated to be £200 billion in 2023[xxxi], 40% of which were in cases of preventable cancer. Whilst direct costs are paid by the UK Government through the National Health Service (i.e., funded by the taxpayer), the unseen costs are to individuals and businesses through loss of productivity and the reduction in the quality of life of cancer sufferers…and their families. Cancer affects nearly every member of a family, either directly as a cancer sufferer or as carers, supportive family members or friends. It will place both an emotional and an economic burden on almost every family in the UK at some point in their lives.

Of the four main types of cancer research (basic, translational, clinical and population), basic research generally does not directly involve humans, although for example human tissue samples may be used. Basic research helps inform researchers which new ideas may be worth pursuing as an effective treatment. Scientists experiment with the building blocks of disease, such as cells and blood, to try to understand how cancer works and to study and develop new drugs and treatments.

Translational research seeks to accelerate the application of discoveries in the laboratory into clinical practice. This is often described by researchers as moving advances in research from 'bench to bedside'. Translational research aims to take what has been learned in basic research and apply that in the development of solutions to the research problem.

Population research is different in that researchers, known as epidemiologists, look for statistical patterns and trends to work out how and why cancers occur in groups of people (populations). Epidemiologists study the patterns, causes, and effects of health and diseases in defined groups. Population research is highly collaborative and can span the spectrum from basic to clinical research.

Clinical research takes these ideas and solutions and studies them in clinical trials. Clinical research involves clinical trials that study a particular group of patients who have been diagnosed with a specific cancer or types of cancer.

This is where the public can participate and be involved.

There is now a far better appreciation of how amplifying the lived experience of anyone who has survived cancer, or someone who has supported a cancer sufferer, can significantly improve the way that research into cancer is conducted[xxxii]. Cancer research needs public participation and involvement if researchers are to progress their research. The demand for cancer patients, survivors, their carers or family members, or even just interested members of the public to become involved in cancer research is increasing, but recruitment in both areas faces severe challenges. The successful recruitment of more, and more diverse, trial participants and advocates requires a better understanding by the public of what 'participation' and 'involvement' in cancer research actually mean if recruitment and retention aspirations are to be met.

The two roles are very different:

- **Participation**: Being involved in a cancer research trial as a participant means having research done to, about or for you (for example, by agreeing to take a new drug to try to cure your cancer).

- **Involvement**: Being involved means collaborating alongside researchers throughout all stages of the research trial process, advocating from a lay perspective. Activities include research advisory groups and committees, focus groups, grant reviews, steering committees, clinical trial protocol reviews, patient information sheets and informed consent reviews, ethics committees, research grant committees, engagement in public dissemination of trial results and even as co-applicants for funding.

There is clearly only one role for a participant in a cancer research trial, but there are many areas in which the public can be involved, bringing different levels of advocacy into different stages of each and every trial. Put simply, **participating** in a cancer research trial is a passive role whereas being **involved** in cancer research is very much an active one.

2: Participation

Clinical research is the comprehensive study of the safety and effectiveness of promising advances in patient care. People are asked to volunteer to test new drugs and treatments to help researchers better understand the impact of the medicine on their condition and health[xxxiii]. Every device, drug, diagnostic test, treatment technique and technology used in medicine today was once tested in or on volunteers who took part in clinical research studies—they were all trial participants. There are two types of studies:

- Observational studies aim to identify and analyse patterns in medical data or in biological samples, such as tissue or blood samples provided by trial participants.
- Clinical trials (also called interventional studies) test the safety and effectiveness of medical interventions, such as medications, procedures and tools, on trial participants.

Clinical trials need people of every age, health status, race, gender, ethnicity and cultural background to participate. By expanding the pool of patients from whom data is gathered, researchers are more likely to be able to recruit the right number and the right profile of patients for a trial. The trial results will then better reflect the realities of society, thus more accurately directing scientific progress and drug discovery. For example, the challenge of age homogeneity in clinical research will only increase as the global population ages. If a drug is not tested on all relevant age groups, there is a risk that treatments could, for example, negatively interact with concomitant treatment or medications common to older adults (comorbidity), or negatively impact patients with underlying conditions more common in younger generations[xxxiv], thus distorting trial results.

Patient participation starts with the identification of the right number and the right profile for a specific trial. Once established recruitment can begin.

RECRUITMENT

COHORT

The actual number of patients required for a clinical research trial will statistically depend upon a number of factors[xxxv], including the research question, the type of trial (Phase 0-4), the prevalence of the particular cancer under study, and the expected dropout rate of patients during the trial (patient survival rates depend upon, for example, the type of cancer, the age of the participants and any comorbidities).

The sample size estimation will need to allow for any adjustment as a result of unplanned interim analysis, planned interim analysis and adjustment for covariates. The sample size is one of the critical steps in planning a clinical trial and any negligence in its estimation may lead to the incorrect rejection of an efficacious drug or conversely may result in an ineffective drug actually getting approval.

STRATEGY

A detailed recruitment strategy will be tailored to the specific research question[xxxvi]. There are a number of recruitment strategies, but generally they are one of the following:

- all patients were recruited all at once and started the trial simultaneously,
- patients enter the trial in a 'batch' mode,
- patients recruited continuously until the desired sample size is achieved, or
- patients are continuously recruited until a fixed date is reached.

SOURCE

Having determined how many patients are needed, and the required cohort profile, it is important for researchers to consider the likely source of patients[xxxvii]. Will the patients be the principal investigator's patients, will they be from a colleague's patient list at the same site or will they be from external sites? Depending upon the trial phase, the probability is that one surgeon alone may not have enough recruitable patients and will therefore need to explore collaboration with other surgeons, possibly even at other locations. The plausibility and feasibility of the study, and patient recruitment, would then have to be discussed with the collaborating surgeons.

PILOT STUDY

Initiating a pilot among these collaborating investigators before a trial begins can give some indication of the likely accrual rate and, at the same time, identify potential barriers. The objectives of a pilot study are to assess the feasibility of the study, identify the site and investigator-specific problems, determine the probability of adherence by the patients and investigators to the study protocol, obtain an estimate of patient follow-up and dropouts, and collect preliminary data for sample size calculation of the full trial. Patients are unlikely to enter studies that they find difficult to understand and/or require multiple follow-ups[xxxviii]. Likewise, investigators may not want to participate in studies that are overly complex and require them to spend excessive hours on paperwork. Therefore, when designing a trial, consideration must be made for the length and complexity of the trial from both the patient's and the investigator's perspectives.

RELEVANCE

Equally important is the need for the investigators to clearly articulate the relevance of the study to the appropriate stakeholders i.e. the patients who will submit themselves to the rigours of the trial and the surgeons who will contribute their time and their patients to the study and, in the process, upset their usual routine. The relevance of the study therefore needs to emphasise the perceived benefits to both present and future patients, to the health care system, and to society in general.

HEALTH ECONOMICS

Cancer health economic research is the application of health economics theory and models to cancer prevention and screening, diagnosis, treatment, survivorship, and end-of-life care. Cancer health economics therefore needs to consider factors associated with the organisation, production, delivery and demand for cancer-related care, as well as outcomes such as type, quantity, quality, and cost of care faced by the patient, family, treatment funder, and society.

The scope also includes the development of data, measures and analytic methods specific to the research. Cancer health economics research is multidisciplinary, combining clinical understanding of cancer control and cancer care, with content and methodology expertise related to economic inputs, outcomes, and approaches to measure and analyse them.

The results of cancer health economics research may be used to inform individual decisions or public policy.

BIAS

Researchers have to avoid conscious or unconscious bias when recruiting patients for a trial. For example, a study in 2020 concluded that not only did some researchers view racial and ethnic minorities as 'less promising' participants, but some respondents also even reported withholding trial opportunities from minorities based on these perceptions[xxxix]. Some funders endorsed using tailored recruitment strategies whereas others ignored race as a factor in trial recruitment. The potential for bias and stereotyping among clinical and research professionals recruiting for cancer clinical trials should be considered when designing interventions to get minority enrolment (if appropriate) thus ensuring the right trial recruitment profile.

ENROLMENT

A key determinant of a successful clinical research trial is the effective recruitment and retention of an adequate number of the study population. However, clinical trial professionals experience several challenges with recruitment and retention of trial participants, with nearly 80% of all trials failing to meet their original enrolment deadline and 55% of trials being terminated because of a failure to achieve full enrolment[xl].

An analysis of the reasons for this failure identified the following extensive list of reasons[xli]:

- **Lack of awareness**: Quite simply, people sometimes just don't know what clinical trials are and don't understand the importance of them.

- **Overly stringent protocol**: A trial protocol that asks patients to record too much information, too often, or has a plethora of unnecessary hospital visits.
- **They don't meet the requirements**: Most trials have strict requirements about other conditions, medications, etc. that may prevent interested individuals from joining.
- **Fear**: People are instinctively afraid of the unknown. Patients may be unsure what to expect from a clinical trial and might be worried that their health may actually suffer from participation.
- **Too much travel**: It could be the case that an individual is more than willing to participate, but that the nearest site is a long commute, and they either don't want to or are unable to make that journey.
- **Fear of placebo**: The majority of the general public doesn't understand the different phases of clinical trials and some could be under the impression that all clinical trials have a placebo. It is likely that if they are going to participate, they want to make sure they are getting the new drug. What they probably don't realise is that in most trials—except Phase 1, where healthy volunteers can be used to test dosage levels—the alternative to the new drug is actually the currently recognised standard of treatment.
- **Distrust of 'Big Pharma'**: Some feel drug companies only see trial participants as numbers, and that they are worried only about future profits and bottom lines. They feel researchers are wrongly motivated and are wary of placing their lives in the hands of the industry.
- **Bias**: Negative stories about unethical researchers or companies skewing research results for a desired outcome.
- **'Guinea Pig'**: Nobody wants to be experimented on 'to see what happens'.
- **Lack of awareness**: Doctors are not aware of trials that may be applicable to their patients.
- **The doctor isn't interested in participating**: Even if they are aware, some are not willing to participate because of the time, staff, and resources their participation would require.
- **'They were never asked'**: People cannot participate in a trial if it is not offered to them. Doctors must be willing to actively share and discuss trials with their patients.

- **Lack of assurance**: When evaluating different treatment options, patients want to be told that the proposed treatment is the best possible one for their current condition, and not that it simply 'may or may not work.'
- **Safety**: People have become accustomed to hearing the multitude of possible side effects in drug advertisements for approved drugs. As a result, they may think the worst when it comes to drugs or therapies that are not yet approved for the market.
- **Terminal illness**: A lot of people believe that clinical trials are a last resort and that you must be terminal if you have been asked to participate in one.
- **Cost**: People question who will pay the expenses incurred for their participation.
- **Afraid of opt-out consequences**: Some people fear that if they join a clinical trial and later decide to opt-out, they will receive a lesser standard of care from their doctor.
- **Lack of patient centricity**: Participants should be made to feel that they are being cared for and listened to, and not just being experimented on.
- **Lack of follow-up**: It is very rare for researchers to follow up with the patients after a study to share the results. People likely want to know that their contributions to the research matter.
- **Not a good match**: Occasionally, when a patient is offered a clinical trial, it is for a therapy that offers little for the specifics of their condition. Whilst the trial may be a good fit initially, the specifics of the treatment that the trial is targeting may not be a match to the patient's condition.
- **Tests**: People often think that participation in a clinical trial means that they will have to undergo many rounds of testing and are reluctant to undergo more 'poking and prodding'.
- **Effective treatment**: If a patient's current treatment appears to be delivering positive results, they will most likely be hesitant to switch to an unproven alternative.
- **Good health**: Individuals who are free of disease and otherwise healthy often do not even consider the possibility of participating in clinical trials.
- **Time requirements**: Some individuals elect not to participate in clinical trials because doing so would take up more of their time, whether it be

in the form of additional physician visits, increased travel time to the study site, or time spent recording personal data at home.

- **Unsupportive family**: Family and peer pressure is a powerful thing. If family and friends have negative attitudes about or are otherwise against an individual participating in a trial, there is a good chance they will not agree to participate.

Sometimes these reasons are trial-specific but they can be broadly classified into the following categories[xlii]—issues related to trial design, demographics, accessibility to a hospital, multi-site challenges, physician attitude, socio-economic disparities and trial-related factors.

Understanding and mitigating these concerns is the key to maximising participation recruitment and minimising patient dropout rates.

ELIGIBILITY CRITERIA

Potential trial participants must be carefully screened to ensure that they meet all of the recruitment criteria for any study before they begin. The eligibility criteria are needed to define the study population and ensure the safety of patients, but clinicians and researchers must avoid both an under-estimation of the number of patients needed (by ensuring that enough patients are recruited to ensure that the results can be analysed with a statistical significance), and an over-estimation (by ensuring that not too many patients are recruited to avoid unnecessary over-exposure to the trial drug, it being unethical if too many patients are recruited and thus unnecessarily over-exposed). Getting the numbers right is no easy task with an insufficient accrual of participants being the leading cause of premature termination[xliii] of oncology trials.

BRIEFING

When a patient expresses an interest in a trial or is asked by their doctor if they would be interested in participating in a trial, the doctor or nurse should tell them, in person, about the trial. They should also be given some printed information to take away and read before committing (a patient information sheet). This gives the patient the opportunity to read about the trial and then come back with any questions that they feel have not been adequately explained. If the patient agrees to take part[xliv], they will usually be randomly assigned to either the treatment group, where they will be given the treatment being assessed, or to the control group, where they will be given an existing standard treatment (or a placebo if no proven standard treatment currently exists).

Whilst the treatments are different in the two (or more) groups, researchers try to keep as many of the other conditions the same as possible. For example, the groups should have people of a similar age, with a similar proportion of men and women (if relevant), who are in similar overall health. In most trials, a computer will be used to randomly decide which group each patient will be allocated to. Many trials are set up so nobody knows who has been allocated to receive which treatment. This is known as 'blinding', and it helps reduce the effects of bias when comparing the outcomes of the treatments. The patient will be asked to sign an 'informed consent' form before actual participation in the trial can begin.

RETENTION

Cancer research trials often involve complex studies with frequent hospital visits, complex medication routines (especially for those patients with comorbidities) and perhaps mandatory biopsies, increasing the burden on patients and decreasing their interest in trial participation. Patients experiencing issues with the regime may decide to stop taking part, especially if, for example, their condition is getting worse or feel the treatment is not helping in any way. Patients can also choose to leave at any point without giving a reason and without affecting the standard of care received. Having a clearly defined patient retention strategy can therefore be considered as important as having a clearly defined recruitment strategy.

There are a variety of strategies to reduce consent withdrawal in clinical trials, such as clear communication, patient-centred approaches, adequate support services, research team flexibility, and early interventions when a patient for example struggles with the logistics of a study.

END OF TRIAL

At the end of the trial, the researchers will publish the results and make them available to anyone who took part and wants to know the results (If the researchers do not offer you the results and you want to know, feel free to ask for them!).

SYNOPSIS

Patient recruitment for participation as a patient on a cancer research trial is the responsibility of the research team. Any researcher planning to conduct clinical research needs to consider the issues of patient recruitment well ahead of time and plan different strategies to avoid or minimise the potential difficulties at the different stages of their study. It is important that the correct numbers and profiles of patients are recruited for trials to ensure that the trial results are unbiased. Patient recruitment is an issue and patient retention in trials can also be problematic.

3: Involvement

RATIONALE

The need for patients to participate in trials is clear and obvious, but why the drive to have patient and public involvement in research?

The introduction of patient and public opinion into research integrates two valuable and powerful viewpoints—the experiential disease and treatment knowledge of the patient, and the professional knowledge of the researcher—which, when combined, not only provides a deeper understanding of the relevance of patient requirements, but also enables the synthesis of priorities for diagnostic and treatment advances. Patient and public involvement provides economic top-quality patient-centred outcomes with high levels of credibility, transparency and accountability in the cancer research decision-making process.

Cancer patients and the public bring unique perspectives into cancer research, making the research more appropriate to and for their needs rather than just being based upon a 'eureka' moment by a researcher. According to the NHS public involvement in research is 'an intrinsic part of citizenship, public accountability and transparency'[xlv].

JUSTIFICATION

The justification for patient and public involvement in cancer research takes many forms:

- **Economic**: An experiential understanding of the diverse needs and priorities of the patient population which, when balanced against the requirements of the researchers, will lead to economic, patient-centred outcomes with high levels of credibility, transparency and accountability.

- **Emancipatory**: *Nihil de nobis, sine nobis* (Nothing about us, without us) is a slogan used to communicate the idea that no policy should be decided by any representative without the full and direct participation of any member of the group affected by that policy. This emancipatory idea for research first emerged in the 1990s during a period of disability activism but lately, the phrase has become adopted by many special interest groups (SIGs). Advocacy input into setting research priorities has, for example, had a positive impact on the amount of research conducted on rare conditions in addition to helping shape the research agenda for more common conditions. Rare cancers had historically tended to suffer from being *a voice seldom heard* when discussions about fund-raising and research grant allocations were being held. Such advocate input now ensures, as a minimum, that each and every one of those voices is heard (even if the outcome is often in favour of the more common cancers due to health economics).

- **Ethical**: In 1996, the Bristol Heart Children Action Group (BHAG) was set up by Helen Rickard following the death of her daughter Samantha. BHAG was responsible for raising awareness of an emerging scandal over body part retention at the Bristol Royal Infirmary (BRI). However, it was only when a public enquiry opened in 1999 that the general public became aware that the issue was far wider. It emerged that the Alder Hey Children's Hospital in Liverpool, as well as other hospitals operating within the National Health Service (NHS), were retaining patients' organs without family consent. In January 2001, the official Alder Hey report was published; it revealed that over 100,000 organs, body parts and entire bodies of foetuses and still-born babies were stored in 210 NHS facilities and that 480,600 samples of tissue taken from dead patients were also being held.

  Subsequently, it also emerged that Birmingham Children's Hospital and Alder Hey had transferred thymus glands that had been removed from live children to a pharmaceutical company for research in return for financial donations. Following the ensuing public enquiry the Human Tissue Act 2004 was enacted in parliament[xlvi] which both consolidated previous legislation and created the Human Tissue Authority (HTA) to 'regulate the removal, storage, use and disposal of human bodies, organs and tissue' for a number of scheduled purposes such as research, transplantation, education and training. The HTA's aim was to build the confidence people have in its regulation by ensuring that human tissue and organs would be used safely, ethically and with proper consent, including for research purposes.

- **Experiential**: It is argued that only those who have shared in, and been part of, a particular experience can properly understand what it is like. Patients and the public, working in collaboration or co-production with researchers in the provision of research, have increased both the quality and relevance of research delivery. With the early involvement of patients and the public, listening to their experiences, challenges, and burdens, and with an honest exchange of information and opinion, researchers can achieve greater levels of empathy and understanding of patient needs which in turn can help shape and prioritise the future of cancer research delivery.

- **International Policy**: The World Health Organisation (WHO) Declaration of Alma-Ata, USSR (1978)[xlvii] stated that 'people have the right and duty to participate individually and collectively in the planning, implementation, and delivery of their health care'. The Global Conference on Primary Health Care in Astana, Kazakhstan (2018)[xlviii] endorsed a new WHO declaration emphasising the critical role of primary health care around the world, reaffirming the commitment expressed in the 1978 Declaration.

- **Methodological**: Patient and public involvement can improve the overall design of trials. Active involvement in qualitative data analysis has been identified as improving the interpretation of findings through the drawing out of relevant themes. Patient and public involvement is important for methodological research as it helps increase the value, integrity and quality of research.

- **Moral**: A clear case for patient and public involvement is laid out as the right of citizens to have a voice in the way that public services spend the money generated from their taxes, their employer's contributions, or simply from their donations. The moral argument is founded on the notion of rights and citizenship.

- **National Policy**: NHS England published a comprehensive document[xlix] in 2017 outlining its position on patient and public involvement in all of its work and how it intends to achieve this. This national policy encourages public and patient involvement in research, with the National Health Service (NHS), the National Institute for Health Research (NIHR) and other research funding bodies all requiring researchers to have already undertaken some form of patient and public involvement— or to at least present a plan for involvement in the proposed research. If they do not intend to involve patients or the public in their research they must explain why or risk losing (or not getting) their funding.

Patient and public involvement should therefore be perceived as a deductive, dynamic, democratic relationship opportunity between the public and health professionals, where people directly or indirectly affected by clinical interventions and research studies have the right to say how they are treated, and to prioritise what and how research is undertaken, with the overarching ambition of developing a more inclusive research environment.

PATIENT AND PUBLIC INVOLVEMENT

A patient or member of the public, an 'advocate', is a person with lived experience either as a patient with cancer, a cancer survivor, an informal carer of a person with cancer, or a member of the general public, who is engaged in advancing something larger for themselves and their community, including increasing awareness, accessing resources, and advancing research into cancer[l]. Patients and the public have a history of proactive involvement in helping to shape cancer research, generally for the benefit of future cancer patients rather than themselves.

This advocacy adds a unique perspective that enables the integration of two valuable and powerful viewpoints, the experiential disease and treatment knowledge, needs and priorities of the patient, and the professional disease and treatment knowledge and priorities of the researcher or clinician. Such a synergistic combination is a key enabler for focused and relevant diagnostic and treatment advances in cancer research.

RATIONALE

There are a number of reasons why clinical trials fail, including the efficacy of the drug, ineffective treatment, safety concerns, poor trial design, and recruitment and retention challenges[li]. Whilst the drug itself may be a reason for a trial's termination, many of these risks could be avoided or minimised by the earlier inclusion of advocacy in a trial. Advocacy helps design and develop research that answers patients' questions, addresses patients' unmet needs, and provides a different perspective into the basic design and parameters of a research project by discussing, understanding and resolving questions such as:

- the differences between existing treatments and the anticipated research outcomes, and how that benefits or impacts the patient;
- how the trial will improve patient outcomes long term;
- how the trial will reduce the patient treatment burden;
- if the trial outcome will be accessible across the wider health landscape;
- if it is feasible to roll out new treatments nationwide;
- the health economics of the trial, for example, the cost of the new treatment to the treatment provider in terms of medicines, equipment, training, and human resources, when compared with the benefits to the patient and society.

Patients and the public should ideally be actively involved in a research study starting from the original research question through to the conclusion of the study, to ensure an equitable and democratic collaboration with the research team. Bringing and maintaining this valuable advocacy perspective into the study, from the initial prioritising of the research question, through the funding application, during the life of the study and then to the dissemination of the study results will ensure that patient and public input is 'not only done but seen to be done'.

For example, the early input of advocacy in the design of lay summaries and patient information sheets can have a significantly positive impact on the recruitment of participants into trials by ensuring that protocols and participant information are both relevant and understandable to the patient.

Patient and public involvement has been shown to raise issues not previously identified or considered by researchers and at the same time, challenges scientists to think more about the service user perspective within their deliberations.

GUIDELINES

Patient and public involvement implies a process of empowerment to inspire the design and delivery of care to cancer patients for specific disease-centred diagnostic and therapeutic care. The National Institute for Health and Care

Research (NIHR) has published guidelines for patient and public involvement in cancer research in the UK[lii]. The standards are designed to:

- be a framework for what good patient and public involvement in research looks like,
- be adaptable to different and changing situations,
- be used with any method or approach to public involvement in research,
- be a tool to help researchers and organisations identify what they are doing well and what needs improving, and
- to encourage reflection and learning, including the sharing of lessons learned when patient and public involvement has failed to lead to expected outcomes.

There is a whole range of different areas where patients and public contributors can be integrated into cancer research studies. However, communication between advocates and the researchers is a two-way process; it must be consistent and meaningful and respect both the researcher's and the advocate's points of view. Communication and mutual respect are therefore the key elements of successful patient and public involvement in research.

SCOPE

The different levels of advocacy in research range from information provision to co-design and empowerment. Different research teams may also have different expectations of advocacy input into the different trial stages. There are five levels of advocacy in cancer research:

- **Level 1-Inform**: Basic information sharing through open access opportunities where people choose to attend or be involved in engagement opportunities such as newsletters, websites or open (public) events where trial results are shared.
- **Level 2-Consult**: Once-off consultation in projects or activities e.g., through surveys, discussion groups or consultation events.
- **Level 3-Collaborate**: Regular involvement over a period of time e.g., focus groups, workshops or the development of patient-facing documents such as Patient Information Sheets or Informed Consent Forms.

- **Level 4-Partner**: Roles that demonstrate partnership. These roles have variable requirements, different natures of activities and different levels of input such as executive members of research advisory groups or steering committees.
- **Level 5-Empower**: Roles that demonstrate strategic and accountable leadership. These roles also have variable requirements, and different levels of input, such as strategic & accountable decision-making activities, or members of groups that make recommendations to committees that have delegated authority from, for example, the board level.

The aim of defining the scope for each level is to ensure that, whatever the level of advocacy, both researchers and advocates are clear on the scope at each level to manage expectations and ensure consistency of understanding (see Table 3).

The role of participation is also included in the table for comparison purposes.

Scope	Advocacy					Participation
	Inform	Consult	Collaborate	Partner	Empower	
	Level 1	Level 2	Level 3	Level 4	Level 5	
Researcher	To provide information, listen and answer questions honestly	To seek advocate input on an ad hoc basis	To include advocates by working jointly with advocates in research development	To partner equally with advocates in research	To follow the advocate lead and support advocate decisions	To act ethically and respectfully in the conduct of research
Advocate	To learn about how to get involved, what's happening in research, and to ask questions	To provide feedback and advice on research activities and questions	To work directly with a researcher or research team throughout a trial	To co-partner on an equal footing with researchers in all aspects of research	To make decisions and lead research activities	To act as a subject in a research study
Process (Examples)	Orientation and information sessions, websites and media campaigns in an open environment	Focus groups, priority-setting activities and as ad hoc members of working groups, discussion groups or expert panels	Standing members of working groups, focus groups, and research advisory committees. Development of patient-facing documents	Advocates as experience-based co-investigators and research partners, as members of research steering committees.	Through steering committees, RECS, and management teams with advocates as principal investigators	Through quantitative, qualitative or mixed-method research

Table 3: Scope of Advocacy in cancer research trials
(Adapted from:
https://journals.plos.org/plosone/article/figure?id=10.1371/journal.pone.0193579.g001)

Focus groups use group dynamics to get the shared experiences of people who have been treated for the same or similar cancers or treatment processes. The group discusses research proposals to compare an existing treatment with a new proposal. Advisory groups discuss patients' experiential knowledge of existing treatments or review proposed treatment pathways, to reduce the patient burden and thus improve recruitment and reduce patient dropout on a trial. Development groups co-develop or critique patient information sheets and informed consent forms whereas strategy groups discuss the future direction of research from a patient perspective. Trial management committees develop, manage or have oversight of existing and emerging cancer trials.

Figure 6 outlines the main areas of advocacy.

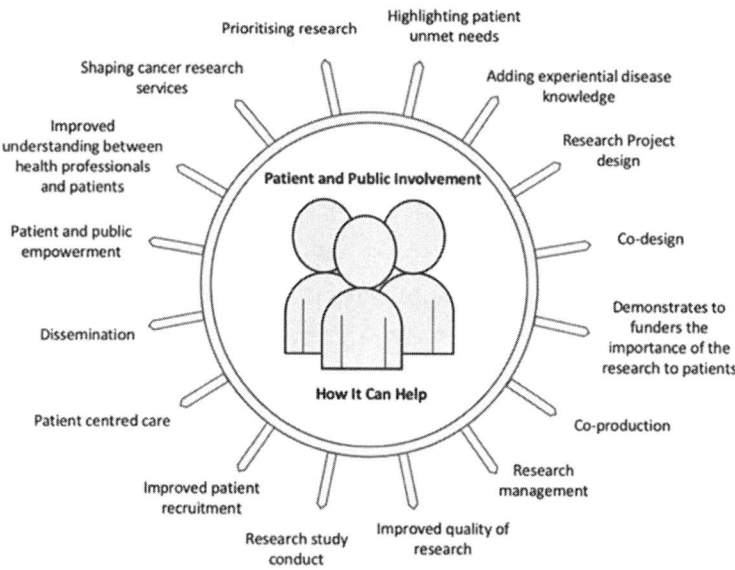

Figure 6: Typical Advocacy Input (Reproduced courtesy Martin Lee)

As the level of advocacy increases in a research trial so does the influence that the advocate has.

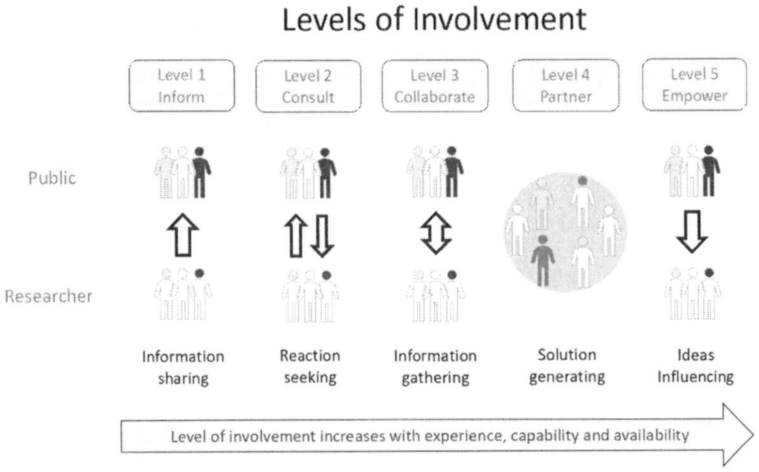

Levels of Involvement

Level 1 Inform	Level 2 Consult	Level 3 Collaborate	Level 4 Partner	Level 5 Empower

Public

Researcher

Information sharing	Reaction seeking	Information gathering	Solution generating	Ideas Influencing

Level of involvement increases with experience, capability and availability

Figure 7: Typical Advocacy Involvement

But this comes with a cost to the advocate! The time commitment for an advocate typically ranges from a couple of hours intermittently at level 1 to sometimes a full-on commitment of many hours per week if a research trial is reaching a critical stage (such as a multi-million pound time-limited grant application that an advocate is a co-applicant on). But, of course, researchers will only involve advocates if they have already committed that time and energy, and advocates will have only been asked if they have indicated a willingness to get that deeply involved.

RECRUITMENT

The number of investigational drugs targeting cancer has nearly quadrupled since the turn of the century, up from 421 to over 1800 today[liii] but experienced cancer research advocates remain a scarce commodity in the cancer research world. Because of this shortage of advocates and the increase in numbers, complexity and duration of cancer trials, there is sometimes a tendency for researchers to call upon advocates that they have been involved with before and trust. This 'familiarity' approach, whilst understandable and expedient in the short term, will not help advocacy or cancer research in the long term.

New advocates are needed to increase both the numbers available, and to increase the diversity of advocates. If cancer trials in the future are to include a truly representative cross-section of advocates, a different approach to recruitment must be considered, starting with increasing the understanding of cancer research advocacy.

Advocate recruitment for a cancer research trial is the responsibility of the research team. Any researcher planning to conduct clinical research needs to consider the issues of advocacy well ahead of time and plan different strategies to minimise and avoid potential difficulties at the different stages of their study. It is important that the correct numbers and profile of advocates are recruited onto trials to ensure continuity during the trial.

SYNOPSIS

Patient and public involvement in the health industry is not new. Indeed, patients and the public have worked alongside researchers for decades to influence research, promote and raise public awareness of their disease, and as participants in research studies, translate and advance new research into more effective, patient-friendly and economical treatments and therapies. However, whilst participation in research trials has always been a clear and fundamental necessity, it is only relatively recently that the full understanding of the value of patient and public advocacy in research trials is being acknowledged and capitalised upon.

4: ENGAGEMENT

Being 'engaged' in cancer research activities is also one of the advocacy roles. However, rather than concentrating on the development of the research trial itself, engagement activities tend to focus on the interface with the general public. Engagement activities include[liv]:

- the sharing of trial results with patient participants and the general public,
- raising awareness and educating the general public about cancer issues,
- addressing legislative and regulatory issues and policies affecting cancer research,
- coordinating or supporting cancer support groups,
- become involved in fund-raising for cancer research, and
- speaking with community groups about the importance of cancer research, trial participation and advocacy.

Engagement activities generally involve a professional media relations expert communicating with the general public. Promotion of the research centre and improving understanding of the roles and opportunities are the prime focus. There are relatively few advocacy activities in 'engagement'.

Participation Advocacy and Engagement in Cancer Research

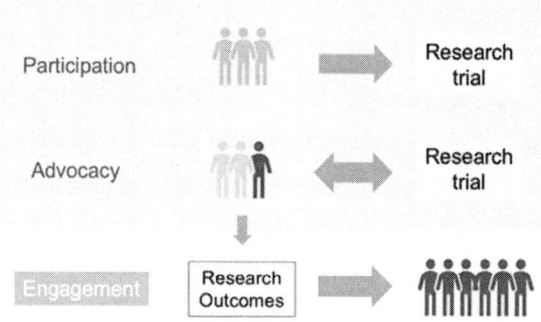

Figure 8: Participation Advocacy and Engagement in Cancer Research

5: SUMMARY

Sadly, little progress has been made in the search for cancer prevention, although the impact of lifestyle changes on cancer is showing promising results[lv]. Cancer research trials therefore tend to focus on finding curative or palliative solutions to enhance the quality of life for patients diagnosed with cancer rather than prevention of the disease.

Participation in a research trial will, by definition, almost always only involve those patients unfortunate enough to have been diagnosed with some form of cancer—although some healthy patients may be asked to volunteer in some specific trials. Agreement to participate is perhaps a way of 'giving back', a tangible 'thank you' to the clinicians. Others may enter because sadly, there is currently little hope of a cure. However, the recruitment of representative groups of participants in trials still remains a challenge.

Research ideas and the necessary funding will continue to materialise, mostly due to the generosity of the public. Combining that with the increasing recognition that patient and public input is essential if the research idea is to be both focused and fruitful, an inevitable increase in demand for more, and more representative, advocates is emerging. With that demand comes the recognition that there also needs to be a shift away from the typical financially secure, white, middle-class, well-educated older advocate of today towards a more representative advocacy cadre capable of ensuring that all voices are heard—in all areas of cancer research. This is not to say that the current group of patient advocates do not have a role to play—far from it. Cancer research would not be where it is today without their past and present input and it is towards them that researchers will inevitably continue to lean—until and unless a new, more diverse group can be recruited and established.

Engagement is different, it involves an outward, rather than an inward, facing perspective where cancer research is discussed in general terms with the public.

CONCLUSION

Cancer diagnosis rates worldwide are now over 20 million per annum. These rates will continue to rise as the population ages. Preventing cancer is an enormous challenge and so cancer research tends to focus on care and cure, with a worldwide annual spend on cancer research of over $5 billion per annum. However, it can take up to 17 years from starting preclinical research to treatment becoming standard of care. In every stage of that process, some form of patient and public input is sought.

Since first becoming involved in patient and public advocacy in 2018, I have been acutely aware, and I am being constantly reminded by cancer researchers, that we need more, and as importantly the right profile of advocates. Advocates are in short supply and recruiting new advocates is challenging.

My aim throughout this book has been to try to reach out to those of you who are perhaps tempted to consider becoming a trial participant or a patient advocate but are not yet convinced that you can make an effective contribution. In actual fact, you are most likely to be the very person that cancer researchers are seeking. By unravelling some of the mysteries of patient and public participation and involvement in cancer research, I hope I have succeeded in convincing you to at least find out more about the subject.

Advocacy is a positive, rewarding and empowering experience. If you are interested in participating or becoming involved in cancer research from a public perspective, start by finding opportunities that match your interests, skills, and abilities. Go online and do some research of your own about the subject, utilise the information listed at the back of this book or make some enquiries at your nearest cancer research hospital.

You might just enjoy the experience; I know I have.

LIST OF ILLUSTRATIONS

Page 91
Figure 8: Participation Advocacy and Engagement in Cancer Research

LIST OF TABLES

GLOSSARY OF TERMS

What does IDK mean?
I Don't Know
Any idea who might?

Anon

Incredibly, I have found one thousand (and one) words, terms and acronyms regularly used in cancer research that may be unfamiliar to lay people. I have therefore included them here and described them in lay terms.

The Institute of Cancer Research Clinical Trials and Statistics Unit (ICR-CTSU) developed a glossary that they colloquially call the 'jargon buster'. The jargon buster was co-developed by advocates and researchers at the ICR-CTSU. It was designed to support advocates and researchers involved in cancer clinical trials at the ICR and covers frequently used terms in cancer research trials. The ICR-CTSU have generously provided me with the contents of that file as the basis for the glossary of terms found in this book. The National Cancer Institute (NCI) in the United States of America also has an extremely comprehensive 'NCI Dictionary of Cancer Terms'[lvi] that I have accessed.

This glossary is a combination of terms from both resources, as well as other terms found during my research. My thanks to them both.

A

Term	Definition
Ablation	In medicine, the removal or destruction of a body part or tissue or its function. Ablation may be performed by surgery, hormones, drugs, radiofrequency, heat, or other methods.
Absolute Risk	The risk of a certain event happening; for example how likely it is that a person will develop cancer over a certain period of time.
Abstract	A brief summary of a longer research paper.
Accelerated Approval	An official process that allows a new drug to be approved by the U.S. Food and Drug Administration (FDA) before it has gone through all of the required levels of testing in humans. It is only used for drugs that treat serious or life-threatening diseases for which other treatments may not be available or may no longer be effective. A drug may be approved through the accelerated approval process if it has shown certain signs in clinical trials that it might be beneficial for patients, such as shrinking a tumour. Further testing of the drug is required after it has received accelerated approval and is on the market, to confirm that it really works. Accelerated approval is one way that patients can receive promising new drugs when other treatment options may not exist. See also International Recognition Procedure.

Term		Definition
Accelerated-fraction Radiation Therapy		Radiation treatment in which the total dose of radiation is divided into small doses and the treatments are given more than once a day. The total dose of radiation is also given over a shorter period of time (fewer days) compared to standard radiation therapy.
Accelerated Radiation Therapy		Radiation treatment in which the total dose of radiation is given over a shorter period of time (fewer days) compared to standard radiation therapy.
Acquired Immunity		A type of immunity that develops when a person's immune system responds to a foreign substance or microorganism, or that occurs after a person receives antibodies from another source. See adaptive and passive immunity.
Action Study		In cancer prevention clinical trials, a study that focuses on determining whether actions people take can prevent cancer.
Active Surveillance		Closely watching a patient's condition but not giving any treatment unless there are changes in test results that show the condition is getting worse. Active surveillance may be used to avoid or delay the need for treatments such as radiation therapy or surgery, which can cause side effects or other problems. During active surveillance, certain exams and tests, such as blood tests, imaging tests, and biopsies, are done on a regular schedule to monitor the condition. It is a type of expectant management.
Acute		Symptoms that start and worsen quickly but do not last over a long time.

Term	Definition
Acute Radiation Sickness	Serious illness caused by being exposed to high doses of certain types of radiation, usually over a short period of time.
Adaptive Immunity	Adaptive immunity occurs in response to being infected with or vaccinated against a microorganism. The body makes an immune response, which can prevent future infection with the microorganism.
Adenine	One of the four nucleotide bases in DNA, with the other three being cytosine (C), guanine (G) and thymine (T). Within a double-stranded DNA molecule, adenine bases on one strand pair with thymine bases on the opposite strand. The sequence of the four nucleotide bases encodes DNA's information.
Adherence	How much a person follows the recommendations from a healthcare provider or the requirements of a clinical trial (for example taking medicine).
Adjuvant	An agent that enhances the activity or therapeutic effect of another pharmacologic substance without having much, if any, therapeutic impact by itself.
Adjuvant Therapy	Treatment given after the main treatment to reduce the chance of cancer coming back. It usually refers to chemotherapy, radiation therapy, hormone therapy, and/or immunotherapy given after surgery.

Term		Definition
Administration of Radioactive Substances Advisory Committee	ARSAC	A committee that reviews research which involves the use of radioactive materials. An ARSAC research certificate is required for all trials involving more radiation exposure than participants would receive in their normal care.
Adoptive Cell Therapy		See T-cell transfer therapy.
Adoptive Cell Transfer		See T-cell transfer therapy.
Advanced Therapy Investigational Medicinal Product	ATIMP	ATMPs are gene therapies, somatic cell therapies and tissue-engineered products (as defined in Article 2(1) of Regulation 1394/2007) which are tested or used in a clinical trial (in accordance with Article 2(d) of Directive 2001/20/EC).

Adverse Event	AE	An adverse event is any untoward medical occurrence (symptom) experienced by a participant who has had treatment within a clinical trial. The event may or may not be related to the trial medicine and may or may not be serious. This is decided by healthcare professionals involved in the trial and leads to Adverse Events (AEs) being reported under the following different categories: • Adverse Reaction (AR) is an AE that is thought to be caused by the trial medicine. • Serious Adverse Event (SAE) is an AE that results in death, is life-threatening, needs admission to hospital, or staying longer in hospital, and results in disability or incapacity or a birth defect. • Serious Adverse Reaction (SAR) is an SAE that is thought to be caused by the trial medicine. • Suspected Unexpected Serious Adverse Reaction (SUSAR) is an SAE that was not expected based on what is already known about the trial medicine.

Term		Definition
		Serious Adverse Reaction (SAR) Adverse Reaction (AR) Unexpected? Suspected Unexpected Serious Adverse Reaction (SUSAR)
Adverse Reaction	AR	Any symptom in a patient that is thought to be related to the trial medicine (see Adverse Event).
Advisory Group		A group that helps to develop, support, advise and monitor clinical services, a research trial or a research facility. The group includes people who use services, carers, researchers and other health and social care professionals.
Advocate		A patient or member of the public who brings the patient and public perspective to the planning, implementation and oversight of clinical and research studies.
Affected Individual		In genetics, a term used to describe a person who has a certain genetic trait or who shows the signs and symptoms of a certain genetic disease.
Agent Study		In cancer prevention, a clinical trial that studies whether taking certain medicines, vitamins, minerals, or food supplements can prevent cancer. Also called a chemo-prevention study.
All-Cause Mortality		The total number of deaths, due to any cause, that occur during a clinical trial.

Term	Definition
Allele	One of two or more versions of DNA sequence (a single base or a segment of bases) at a given genomic location.
	An individual inherits two alleles, one from each parent, for any given genomic location where such variation exists. If the two alleles are the same, the individual is homozygous for that allele. If the alleles are different, the individual is heterozygous.
Allocation Concealment	A technique used to prevent selection bias by concealing the allocation sequence from those assigning participants to intervention groups, until the moment of assignment.
	Allocation concealment prevents researchers from (unconsciously or otherwise) influencing which participants are assigned to a given intervention group.
Alpha-emitter Radiation Therapy	Therapy that uses a radioactive substance that gives off a type of high-energy radiation called an alpha-particle to kill cancer cells.
	The radioactive substance is injected into a vein, travels through the blood, and collects in certain tissues in the body, such as areas of bone with cancer. This type of radiation may cause less damage to nearby healthy tissue.

Term		Definition
Amino Acid		The fundamental molecule that serves as the building block for proteins. There are 20 different amino acids. A protein consists of one or more chains of amino acids (called polypeptides) whose sequence is encoded in a gene. Some amino acids can be synthesised in the body, but others (essential amino acids) cannot and must be obtained from a person's diet.
Anaemia		The condition of not having enough healthy red blood cells or haemoglobin to carry oxygen to the body's tissues.
Anaesthesia		A loss of feeling or awareness caused by drugs or other substances. Anaesthesia keeps patients from feeling pain during surgery or other procedures. Local anaesthesia is a loss of feeling in one small area of the body.
Anaplastic		A term used to describe cancer cells that divide rapidly and have little or no resemblance to normal cells.
Androgen		A male sex hormone such as testosterone.
Aneuploidy		An abnormality in the number of chromosomes in a cell due to loss or duplication. In humans, aneuploidy would be any number of chromosomes other than the usual 46.
Angiogenesis		Angiogenesis is the formation of new blood vessels. It involves the migration, growth, and differentiation of endothelial cells, which line the inside wall of blood vessels. The process of angiogenesis is controlled by chemical signals in the body.
Anonymised		The process of removing all information that could lead to an individual being identified (see Pseudonymised).

Term		Definition
Antibodies		Antibodies are proteins that protect the body when an unwanted substance enters it. Antibodies are produced by the immune system; they bind to unwanted substances in order to eliminate them from your system.
Antibody Therapy		Treatment that uses antibodies to help the body fight cancer, infection, or other diseases. Antibodies are proteins made by the immune system that bind to specific markers on cells or tissues. Monoclonal antibodies are a type of antibody made in the laboratory that can be used in diagnosis or treatment. In cancer treatment, monoclonal antibodies may kill cancer cells directly, they may block the development of tumour blood vessels, or they may help the immune system kill cancer cells.
Anti-cancer Therapy		Treatment to stop or prevent cancer. Types of anti-cancer therapy include chemotherapy, radiation therapy, surgery, immunotherapy, and others.
Anticarcinogenic		Having to do with preventing or delaying the development of cancer.
Anticodon		A trinucleotide sequence located at one end of a transfer RNA (tRNA) molecule, which is complementary to a corresponding codon in a messenger RNA (mRNA) sequence. Each time an amino acid is added to a growing polypeptide during protein synthesis, a tRNA anticodon pairs with its complementary codon on the mRNA molecule, ensuring that the appropriate amino acid is inserted into the polypeptide.

Term		Definition
Antigen		A toxin or other foreign substance which induces an immune response in the body, especially the reproduction of antibodies.
Antigen-Presenting Cell	APC	An immune cell that detects, engulfs and informs the adaptive immune response to an infection. There are three types of APCs: • dendritic cells, • macrophages, and B-cells. APCs can present exogenous antigens to naive or memory T-cells, activating them.
Antisense		The non-coding DNA strand of a gene. In a cell, antisense DNA serves as the template for producing messenger RNA (mRNA), which directs the synthesis of a protein.
Anti-tumour Activity		Activity that destroys or inhibits the growth of cancer cells.
Archival Tumour Tissue (Sample)		Stored tissue that is embedded in paraffin. A great wealth of knowledge has been derived from research work on archival tissue. For example, it has aided in and still contributes to, the discovery of diagnostic and therapeutic tumour markers.
Arm		A group of participants in a clinical trial receiving a specified treatment.

Term		Definition
Artificial Intelligence	AI	The ability of a computer to perform functions that are usually thought of as intelligent human behaviour, such as learning, reasoning, problem-solving, and decision-making. AI uses computer programs that analyse very large amounts of information to learn how to help make decisions or predictions. In medicine, the use of AI may help improve cancer screening and diagnosis, and to plan treatment. It may also be used in research and in drug discovery and development.
Artificial T-cell Receptor		See Chimeric Antigen Receptor.
Asymptomatic		Having no signs or symptoms of a disease.
Audit		A study designed to determine if the quality of a service meets a defined standard.
Authorised Health Professional	AHP	A registered doctor, dentist, nurse or pharmacist.
Autosome		One of the numbered chromosomes, as opposed to the sex chromosomes. Humans have 22 pairs of autosomes and one pair of sex chromosomes (XX or XY). Autosomes are numbered roughly in relation to their sizes. The largest autosome (chromosome 1) has approximately 2,800 genes; the smallest autosome (chromosome 22) has approximately 750 genes.
Auxiliary Medicinal Product	AxMP	A medicinal product used for the needs of a clinical trial as described in the protocol, but not as an investigational medicinal product.

B

Term		Definition
Background Therapy		The current medication taken as a standard of care for a particular disease (see Standard of Care).
Bacteria		Bacteria are small single-celled organisms. The human body is full of bacteria, but most bacteria are harmless, and some are even helpful. A relatively small number of species of bacteria cause disease.
Basal Cell		A small, round cell found in the lower part (base) of the epidermis, the outer layer of the skin.
Basement Membrane		Thin layers of a specialised extracellular matrix that form the supporting structure upon which epithelial and endothelial cells grow.
Base Pair		A base pair consists of two complementary DNA nucleotide bases that pair together to form a 'rung' of the DNA 'ladder'.
Basic Research		Seek to change the practice of oncology through new discoveries and practices that generate new knowledge relevant to the basic biology and causes of human cancers.
Basket Trial		A type of clinical trial that tests how well a new drug or treatment pathway works in patients who have different types of cancer that all have the same mutation or biomarker. In basket trials, patients all receive the same treatment that targets the specific mutation or biomarker found in their cancer. Basket trials may allow new drugs to be tested and approved more quickly than standard clinical trials. Basket trials may also be useful for studying rare cancers and cancers with rare genetic changes. Also called a bucket trial.
B-cell		A type of white blood cell that makes antibodies. B-cells are part of the immune system and develop from stem cells in the bone marrow. Also called b-lymphocyte.

137

Term		Definition
Benign Tumour		A growth that is not cancerous. It is a tumour that does not spread to other parts of the body.
Bias		When a trial's results are affected by factors that are not related to the treatment being tested. Biased results can lead to the wrong conclusions being made about a treatment.
Benign		See Non-malignant.
Bioinformatics		Bioinformatics, as related to genetics and genomics, is a scientific subdiscipline that involves using computer technology to collect, store, analyse and disseminate biological data and information, such as DNA and amino acid sequences or annotations about those sequences. Scientists and clinicians use databases that organise and index such biological information to increase our understanding of health and disease and, in certain cases, as part of medical care.
Biological Activity		The beneficial or adverse effects of a drug on living matter.
Biological Response Modifier	BRM	See Biotherapy.
Biological Therapy		See Biotherapy.
Biomarker (short for biological marker)		A substance in the body that doctors can measure to help them tell how a disease is developing or a treatment is working. Also called a signature molecule and molecular marker.
Biomedical Research Centre	BRC	Partnerships between universities and NHS organisations. BRCs bring together researchers and doctors to turn lab-based research into new treatments, diagnostics and medical technologies.
Biopsy		The removal of a small amount of tissue to either examine under a microscope or to carry out different tests.

Term		Definition
Biotherapy		The class of medications that target the disease-causing mechanism. Biotherapy is used in autoimmune diseases as first-line medications or after the failure of conventional agents. Also called biological response modifier, biological therapy or immunotherapy.
Bispecific Antibody		A type of antibody that can bind to two different antigens at the same time. Bispecific antibodies are being studied in the imaging and treatment of cancer. They are made in the laboratory.
Blinding		The practice of keeping the trial participants, care providers, those collecting data, and sometimes even those analysing data unaware of which intervention is being administered to which participant. Blinding is intended to prevent bias on the part of study personnel. Also called masking.
Blinded Study		A type of study in which patients (single-blind) or both the patients and the researchers (double-blind) who are involved in a clinical study do not know which drug or treatment the patient is being given. The opposite of a blinded study is an open-label study.
B-lymphocyte		See B-cell.
Bone Marrow Suppression		When fewer blood cells are made in the bone marrow. It is a common side effect of some strong medicines, such as chemotherapy. Bone marrow suppression can cause anaemia.
Bone Metastasis		Cancer that has spread from the original (primary) site to the bone.
Bone Seeking Radioisotope		A radioactive substance that is given through a vein and then collects in bone cells and tumour cells that have spread to the bone. It kills cancer cells by giving off low-level radiation.
Brachytherapy		Treatment where a small radioactive material (a source) is put inside or close to a cancer tumour. Also called internal radiation therapy.

Term		Definition
Bradford Hill Criteria		A group of nine principles that can be useful in establishing epidemiologic evidence of a causal relationship between a presumed cause and an observed effect. The criteria are: • strength (effect size), • consistency (reproducibility), • specificity, • temporality, • biological gradient (dose-response relationship), • plausibility, • coherence, • experiment, and • analogy.
British Association of Cancer Research	BAC R	A professional membership association for all those working and studying in cancer research in the United Kingdom and beyond.
Bucket Trial		See Basket Trial.

C

Term		Definition
Cancer		A group of diseases where cells grow uncontrollably. They can go beyond their usual boundaries to invade nearby tissues and can spread to other organs. Cancer can begin almost anywhere in the body.
Cancer Cluster		The emergence of a larger-than-expected number of cases of cancer in a geographic area over a certain period of time.
Cancer of Unknown Primary	CUP	Where cancer cells are found in the body but the location where the cells first started to grow (the origin, or primary site) cannot be determined. Also called carcinoma of unknown primary (origin).
Cancer-Predisposing Gene Mutation		The term used to describe mutations (changes) in certain genes that may increase a person's risk of some types of cancer. For example, a person who has certain mutations in the BRCA1 or BRCA2 gene has higher-than-normal risks of developing breast and ovarian cancer. Cancer-predisposing gene mutations are usually inherited (passed from parent to child) and may be seen within families. Knowing if a person has a cancer-predisposing gene mutation may help prevent, diagnose, and treat cancer. Not all people who have a cancer-predisposing gene mutation will develop cancer. Also called cancer susceptibility gene mutation.
Cancer Research		Research to develop safe and effective methods to prevent, detect, diagnose, treat, and, ultimately, cure the collection of diseases called cancer.
Cancer Research UK	CRUK	The world's largest independent cancer research organisation.
Cancer Susceptibility Gene Mutation		See Cancer-Predisposing Gene Mutation.

Term		Definition
Candidate Gene		A gene that is believed to be related to a particular trait, such as a disease or a physical attribute. Because of its genomic location or its known function, the gene is suspected to play a role in that trait, thus making it a candidate for additional study.
Carcinogen		Any substance that causes cancer or increases the risk of cancer.
Carcinoma		Cancer that begins in the skin or in tissues that line or cover internal organs.
Carcinoma in situ		A condition in which abnormal cells that look like cancer cells under a microscope are found only in the place where they first formed and haven't spread to nearby tissue. At some point, these cells may become cancerous and spread into nearby normal tissue. There are many different types of carcinoma in situ depending on the type of tissue in which it began.
Carcinoma of Unknown Primary (Origin)	CUP	See Cancer of Unknown Primary.
Cardiovascular Effects		These are side effects, such as high blood pressure, abnormal heart rhythms, and heart failure, that can be caused or exacerbated by chemotherapy and radiation therapy, as well as by newer forms of cancer treatment, such as targeted therapies and immunotherapies.
Carer		A person who gives care to people who need help taking care of themselves. Carers may be health professionals, family members, friends, social workers, or members of the clergy. They may give care at home or in a hospital or other health care setting.

Term		Definition
Carrier		A carrier, as related to genetics, is an individual who 'carries' and can pass on to its offspring a genomic variant (allele) associated with a disease (or trait) that is inherited in an autosomal recessive or sex-linked manner, and who does not show symptoms of that disease (or features of that trait). The carrier has inherited the variant allele from one parent and a normal allele from the other parent. Any offspring of carriers is at risk of inheriting a variant allele from their parents, which would result in that child having the disease (or trait).
Carrier Screening		Carrier screening involves testing to see if a person 'carries' a genetic variation (allele) associated with a specific disease or trait. A carrier has inherited a normal and a variant allele for a disease- or trait-associated gene, one from each parent. Most typically, carrier screening is performed to look for recessively inherited diseases when the suspected carrier has no symptoms of the disease, but that person's offspring could have the disease if the other parent is a carrier of a harmful variant in the same gene.
Case-control Study		A study that compares two groups of people: • those with the disease or condition under study (cases), and • a very similar group of people who do not have the disease or condition (controls). Researchers study the medical and lifestyle histories of the people in each group to learn what factors may be associated with the disease or condition. For example, one group may have been exposed to a particular substance that the other was not. Also called a retrospective study.
Case Report Form	CRF	A document which records all the information collected for each trial participant.

Term		Definition
Castration-resistant Prostate Cancer	CR PC	Prostate cancer that keeps growing even when the amount of testosterone in the body is reduced to very low levels. Many early-stage prostate cancers need normal levels of testosterone to grow, but castration-resistant prostate cancers do not.
Castration-sensitive Prostate Cancer		Prostate cancer that needs androgens (male hormones) to grow and therefore stops growing when androgens are not present. Many early-stage prostate cancers are androgen-dependent, thus reducing the amount of androgens in the body or blocking their action may be an effective type of therapy.
Cell-cell Signalling		The transfer of information from one cell to another. Cells signal each other by direct contact with each other or by the release of a substance from one cell that is taken up by another cell. Intercellular communication is important for cells to grow and work normally. Cells that lose the ability to respond to signals from other cells may become cancer cells. Also called cell-cell signalling and cell-to-cell signalling.
Cell-free DNA Testing		A laboratory method that involves analysing free (i.e., non-cellular) DNA contained within a biological sample, most often to look for genomic variants associated with a hereditary or genetic disorder. Cell-free DNA testing is used for the detection and characterisation of some cancers and to monitor cancer therapy.
Cell-mediated Immunity		Cell-mediated immunity (or cellular immunity) is an immune response that does not involve antibodies.
Cells		Cells are the basic building blocks of all living things. The human body is composed of trillions of cells. They provide structure for the body, take in nutrients from food, convert those nutrients into energy, and carry out specialised functions.

Term	Definition
Cell Signalling	See Signal Transduction.
Cell-to-cell Signalling	See Intercellular communication.
Cellular Adoptive Immunotherapy	See T-cell Transfer Therapy.
Centromere	A constricted region of a chromosome that plays a key role in helping the cell divide up its DNA during division (mitosis and meiosis). Specifically, it is the region where the cell's spindle fibres attach. Following the attachment of the spindle fibres to the centromere, the two identical sister chromatids that make up the replicated chromosome are pulled to opposite sides of the dividing cell, such that the two resulting daughter cells end up with identical DNA.
Checkpoint Inhibitors	Checkpoint inhibitors are a type of immunotherapy. They are a treatment for cancers such as skin cancer and lung cancer. These drugs block different checkpoint proteins.
Chemo brain	A term commonly used to describe thinking and memory problems that a patient with cancer may have before, during, or after cancer treatment. Signs and symptoms of 'chemo brain' include disorganised behaviour or thinking, confusion, memory loss, and trouble concentrating, paying attention, learning, and making decisions. Chemo brain may be caused by the cancer itself (such as a brain tumour) or by cancer treatment, such as chemotherapy and other anti-cancer drugs, radiation therapy, hormone therapy, and surgery. It may also be caused by conditions related to cancer treatment, such as anaemia, fatigue, infection, pain, hormone changes, sleep problems, nutrition problems, stress, anxiety, and depression. Chemo brain may last for a short time or for many years.

Term		Definition
Chemo-immunotherapy		Chemotherapy combined with immunotherapy. Chemotherapy uses different drugs to kill or slow the growth of cancer cells; immunotherapy uses treatments to stimulate or restore the ability of the immune system to fight cancer.
Chemo-prevention		The use of certain drugs or other substances to help lower a person's risk of developing cancer or keep it from coming back.
Chemo-prevention Study		See Agent Study.
Chemotherapy		A type of cancer treatment that uses one or more anti-cancer drugs as part of a standardised chemotherapy regimen. Chemotherapy may be given with a curative intent or it may aim to prolong life or to reduce symptoms.
Chief Investigator	CI	A doctor with expert knowledge in the area of research who leads and has overall responsibility for the trial.
Chimeric Antigen Receptor	CAR (T)	Receptor proteins that have been engineered to give T-cells the new ability to target a specific antigen. Also known as chimeric immunoreceptors, chimeric T-cell receptors or artificial T-cell receptors.
Chimeric Immuno-receptor		See Chimeric Antigen Receptor.
Chimeric T-cell Receptor		See Chimeric Antigen Receptor.
Chromosome		A threadlike structure of nucleic acids and proteins found in the nucleus of most living cells, carrying genetic information in the form of genes.
Chronic		A disease or condition that persists, often slowly, over a long period of time.

Term		Definition
Circulating Tumour Marker		A substance, such as a protein or fragment of DNA, that is released into a person's blood, urine, other body fluid, or stool by tumour cells or other cells of the body. Circulating tumour markers may be a sign of cancer or certain benign (non-cancer) conditions. Measurements of circulating tumour marker levels in blood or other body fluid may be used along with results of other tests, such as biopsies and imaging, to help diagnose some types of cancer. Knowing the levels of circulating tumour markers may also help plan cancer treatment, make a likely prognosis, and find out how well treatment is working or if the cancer has come back.
Clinical Research		Research in which people, or data or samples of tissue from people, are studied to understand health and disease. Clinical research helps find new and better ways to detect, diagnose, treat, and prevent disease. Types of clinical research include clinical trials, which test new treatments for a disease, and natural history studies, which collect health information to understand how a disease develops and progresses over time.
Clinical Research Associate		An individual who undertakes monitoring activities for a trial. Also known as a Monitor.
Clinical Researcher		A health professional who works directly with patients, or uses data from patients, to do research on health and disease and to develop new treatments. Clinical researchers may also do research on how health care practices affect health and disease.
Clinical Resistance		The failure of a cancer to shrink after treatment.
Clinical Significance		Clinical significance suggests that the difference between two treatments is clinically important (i.e. one treatment improves medical care significantly more than another).

Term		Definition
Clinical Stage		The stage of cancer (amount or spread of cancer in the body) that is based on tests that are done before surgery. These include physical exams, imaging tests, laboratory tests (such as blood tests), and biopsies.
Clinical Study	CS	A type of research study that tests how well new medical approaches work. Also called a clinical trial.
Clinical Trial	CT	See Clinical Study.
Clinical Trial Authorisation	CTA	Authorisation to run a clinical trial of a medicine by a regulator (the Medicines and Healthcare Products Regulatory Agency [MHRA] in the UK).
Clinical Trial Notification Scheme		For certain 'Type A' trials notification of the trial to the MHRA is possible. Type A trials are those involving medicinal products licensed in any EU Member State if: • they relate to the licensed range of indications, dosage and form, or • they involve off-label use (such as in paediatrics and oncology, etc.) if this off-label use is established practice and supported by sufficient published evidence and/or guidelines.
Clinical Trial of an Investigational Medicinal Product	CTIMP	A study that looks at how safe or effective a medicine is.

Term		Definition
Clinical Trial Phase		A part of the clinical research process that answers specific questions about whether treatments or other interventions that are being studied work and are safe. <ul><li>Phase I trials test the best way to give a new treatment and the best dose.</li><li>Phase II trials test whether a new treatment has an effect on the disease.</li><li>Phase III trials compare the results of people taking a new treatment with the results of people taking the standard treatment.</li><li>Phase IV trials are done using thousands of people after a treatment has been approved and marketed, to check for side effects that were not seen in the phase III trial.</li></ul>
Clinical Trials Regulations	CTR	The laws which specify how clinical trials must be run. In the UK this is the Medicines for Human Use (Clinical Trials) Regulations (SI 2004 1031) and its amendments.
Clinical Trial Sponsor		A person, company, institution, group, or organisation that oversees or pays for a clinical trial and collects and analyses the data. Also called a trial sponsor.
Clinician		A health professional who takes care of patients.
Cloning		Cloning, as it relates to genetics and genomics, involves using scientific methods to make identical, or virtually identical, copies of an organism, cell or DNA sequence. 'Molecular cloning' typically refers to isolating and copying a particular DNA segment of interest for further study.
Cluster Randomised Trial		A trial where individuals are grouped (e.g., by clinics, families, regions) and then randomly assigned to different treatments.
Co-applicant		A person involved in the development of a grant application who has some responsibility for the management and/or delivery of a study. Patient advocates can be involved in a research project or trial as co-applicants.

Term	Definition
Codominance	Codominance, as it relates to genetics, refers to a type of inheritance in which two versions (alleles) of the same gene are expressed separately to yield different traits in an individual. Instead of one trait being dominant over the other, both traits appear, such as in a plant or animal that has more than one pigment colour.
Codon	A DNA or RNA sequence of three nucleotides (a trinucleotide) that forms a unit of genomic information encoding a particular amino acid or signalling the termination of protein synthesis (stop signals). There are 64 different codons: 61 specify amino acids and 3 are used as stop signals.
Cohort	A group of individuals who share a common trait, such as age or illness. In medicine, a cohort is a group that is part of a clinical trial or study and is observed over a period of time.
Cohort Study	A type of study that follows a group of participants over a period of time, looking at how certain factors affect their health.
Combination Therapy	See Multimodality Therapy.
Comorbidity	The presence of two or more medical conditions in a patient at the same time.
Comparator	A treatment or placebo compared against a treatment being investigated in a clinical trial.
Complementary DNA	See copy DNA.
Complex Disease	A complex disease (or condition), when discussed in the context of genetics, is a disorder that results from the contributions of multiple genomic variants and genes in conjunction with significant influences of the physical and social environment. This stands in contrast to a 'simple' genetic disease that is more directly caused by mutations in a single gene. Common examples of complex genetic diseases include heart disease, diabetes, and cancer. Also known as multifactorial diseases.

Term		Definition
Compliance		The act of following a medical regimen or schedule correctly and consistently, including taking medicines or following a diet.
Complication		The act of following a medical regimen or schedule correctly and consistently, including taking medicines or following a diet.
Computed (Axial) Tomography	C(A)T	A scan that uses specialised x-ray equipment to produce cross-sectional images of the body.
Concomitant		Occurring or existing at the same time as something else. In medicine, it may refer to a condition a person has or a medication a person is taking that is not being studied in the clinical trial he or she is taking part in.
Concomitant Treatment		Treatment given at the same time as another treatment.
Concordat		An agreement or treaty.
Confidence Interval		A measure of the uncertainty around the main finding of a statistical analysis. Wider intervals indicate lower precision and narrow intervals indicate greater precision. For example, a 95% confidence interval for an estimated treatment effect indicates that if the same experiment were to be repeated 100 times, the true treatment effect would on average fall in the range of the interval 95 times.
Conformal Radiotherapy		Treatment that delivers a high dose volume of radiotherapy that is shaped to conform to the target volume (tumour) whilst minimising the dose to critical normal tissues in the adjacent area.

Term		Definition
Confounder		A factor that is associated with both a treatment and the outcome of interest. For example, if one treatment group in a controlled trial is younger than the control group, it will be difficult to decide whether a lower risk of death in one group is due to the treatment or the difference in age. Age is then said to be a confounder. Randomisation tries to reduce any difference in confounders between experimental and control groups. Also known as Confounding Variable.
Confounding Variable		See Confounder.
Congenital		A condition or trait that exists at birth. Congenital conditions or traits may be hereditary or result from an action or exposure occurring during pregnancy or at birth, or they may be due to a combination of these factors.
Consent		Permission given by a patient to join a clinical trial or receive a specific treatment.
Consolidation Therapy		See Intensification Therapy.
Contract Research Organisation	CRO	A service organisation that provides support to the pharmaceutical and biotechnology industries (and other organisations) in the form of research services outsourced on a contract basis.
Contra-Indication		A specific circumstance when the use of certain treatments could be harmful.
Contrast Medium		A substance introduced into a part of the body in order to improve the visibility of internal structures during radiography.
Control Arm		The comparison group in a randomised trial. Those in the control group (or arm) will not receive the trial treatment but will provide a comparison to see how the trial treatment compares against no treatment or another known treatment. Also known as control group, study group or treatment group.

Term		Definition
Control Group		See Control Arm
Controlled Clinical Trial		A clinical study that includes a comparison (control) group. The comparison group receives a placebo, another treatment, or no treatment at all. Also called a controlled study.
Controlled Study		See Controlled Clinical Trial.
Coordinated System for gaining NHS Permission	CSP	The CSP is: • a service to Investigators which facilitates set up and approval for research in the NHS, and • a standardised process by which NHS organisations provide NHS permission for research. Also sometimes used informally to refer to the information system which supports the process.
Co-Production		An approach in which researchers, practitioners and the public work together on a project.
Copy DNA	cDNA	cDNA is synthetic DNA that has been transcribed from a specific mRNA through a reaction using the enzyme reverse transcriptase. Whilst DNA is composed of both coding and non-coding sequences, cDNA contains only coding sequences. Scientists often synthesise and use cDNA as a tool in gene cloning and other research experiments. Also called Complementary DNA.
Co-researcher		Someone who researches together with one or more other people. Patient advocates can be involved in a research project as co-researchers.
Co-Sponsor		Where two or more organisations share a significant interest in a study, they may elect to act as co-sponsors.

Term	Definition
Course of Treatment	A treatment plan made up of several cycles of treatment. For example, treatment given for one week followed by three weeks of rest (no treatment) is one treatment cycle. When a treatment cycle is repeated multiple times on a regular schedule, it makes up a course of treatment. A course of treatment can last for several months.
Cross-over Trial	Comparison of treatments in which patients are switched to the other treatment after a certain amount of time.
Cross-sectional Study	A type of research study in which a group of people is observed, or certain information is collected, at a single point in time or over a short period of time; for example, a survey may be carried out to collect information about the total number of people in a group who have or had a certain disease (such as cancer) or risk factor (such as smoking or obesity). This survey may be able to provide some information about whether there is an association between smoking (risk factor) and cancer (disease) but does not prove that they are linked. Results from a cross-sectional study may be used to plan other research studies. A cross-sectional study is a type of observational (epidemiologic) study.
Cum Hoc, Ergo Propter Hoc	Latin *With this, therefore because of this.* The idea that correlation implies causation is an example of a questionable-cause logical fallacy in which two events occurring together are taken to have established a cause-and-effect relationship. The Bradford Hill criteria are a group of nine principles that can be useful in establishing epidemiologic evidence of a causal relationship. See also *post hoc, ergo propter hoc*
Cumulative Dose	In medicine, the total amount of a drug or radiation given to a patient over time; for example, the total dose of radiation given in a series of radiation treatments.

Term	Definition
Cumulative Exposure	The total amount of a substance or radiation that a person is exposed to over time. Cumulative exposure to a harmful substance or radiation may increase the risk of certain diseases or conditions.
Cumulative Risk	A measure of the total risk that a certain event will happen during a given period of time. In cancer research, it is the likelihood that a person who is free of a certain type of cancer will develop that cancer by a specific age.
Curative Surgery	Surgery to remove all malignant (cancerous) tissue, which is meant to cure the disease. This includes removing part or all of the cancerous organ or tissue and a small amount of healthy tissue around it. Nearby lymph nodes may also be removed. Curative surgery works best for localised cancer. Chemotherapy or radiation therapy may be given before surgery to shrink the tumour or after surgery to kill any cancer cells that remain.
Curative Treatment	Treatment that is meant to cure an illness or disease with the goal of a full recovery that includes an acceptable quality of life. For cancer, a curative therapy approach depends on the cancer type and stage.
Cryoablation	See Cryotherapy.
Cryoprobe	A blunt chilled instrument used to freeze tissues in cryosurgery.
Cryosurgery	The use of extreme cold in surgery to destroy abnormal or diseased tissue.
Cryotherapy	The use of extreme cold to freeze and remove abnormal tissue. Doctors use it to treat many skin conditions (including warts and skin tags) and some cancers, including prostate, cervical and liver cancer. Also called cryoablation.
Cytogenetics	A branch of biology focused on the study of chromosomes and their inheritance, especially as applied to medical genetics.

Term	Definition
Cytokines	Cytokines are major regulators of innate and adaptive immunity that enable cells of the immune system to communicate over short distances.
Cytosine	One of the four nucleotide bases in DNA, with the other three being adenine (A), guanine (G) and thymine (T). Within a double-stranded DNA molecule, cytosine bases on one strand pair with guanine bases on the opposite strand. The sequence of the four nucleotide bases encodes DNA's information.
Cytotoxic	Toxic to living cells.
Cytotoxic T-cell	See Killer T-cell.
Cytotoxic T-Lymphocyte	See Killer T-cell.

D

Term		Definition
Data Monitoring Committee	DMC	A committee that may be established by the sponsor to assess at intervals, the progress of a clinical trial, the safety data, and the critical efficacy endpoints, and to recommend to the sponsor whether to continue, modify, or stop a trial.
Data Protection		All personal information is protected in the UK by the Data Protection Act 2018. This means that researchers must protect the confidentiality of the information they collect about research participants.
Data Science		The study of large, complex data sets that arise from various types of research projects. With respect to genomic studies, such work requires expertise in quantitative scientific disciplines such as bioinformatics, computational biology and biostatistics.
Debulking		See Tumour Debulking.
Definitive Diagnosis		A final diagnosis that is made after getting the results of tests, such as blood tests and biopsies, that are done to find out if a certain disease or condition is present.
Deficient DNA Mismatch Repair		See Mismatch Repair.
Deficient Mismatch Repair		See Mismatch Repair.
Delegation Log		A list of appropriately qualified persons to whom the investigator has delegated significant trial-related duties.
Deleterious Mutation		See Predisposing Mutation.

Term		Definition
Deletion		A deletion, as related to genomics, is a type of mutation that involves the loss of one or more nucleotides from a segment of DNA. A deletion can involve the loss of any number of nucleotides, from a single nucleotide to an entire piece of a chromosome.
Dendritic cell	DC	Antigen-presenting cells that inform the body's response to invasive pathogens whilst enforcing tolerance to harmless antigens.
De novo		Latin *of new*. In cancer, the first occurrence of cancer in the body.
De novo Mutation		A term used to describe a change in the DNA sequence of a gene that is seen for the first time in a person and has not appeared in previous generations. A de novo mutation can explain how a person can have a genetic condition that did not occur in his or her parents. A de novo mutation can occur in an egg or sperm cell of a parent, in the fertilised egg soon after the egg and sperm unite, or in another type of cell during embryo development. A person who has a de novo mutation may pass the mutation to his or her child. Some de novo mutations may lead to cancer or other diseases. Also called de novo variant, new mutation, and new variant.
De novo Variant		See De novo Mutation.

Term		Definition
Deoxyribonucleic Acid	DNA	A polymer composed of two polynucleotide chains that coil around each other to form a double helix. The polymer carries genetic instructions for the development, functioning, growth and reproduction of all known organisms and many viruses. DNA and ribonucleic acid are both nucleic acids.
Dependent Variable		A variable whose value depends on that of another; for example the blood pressure of a trial participant that is measured during a study.
Development Safety Update Report	DSUR	The common format for annual safety reports on investigational drugs is the International Conference on Harmonisation (ICH) regions.
Diagnostic Technique		A type of method or test used to help diagnose a disease or condition. Imaging tests and tests to measure blood pressure, pulse, and temperature are examples of diagnostic techniques.
Diagnostic Test		A test used to help determine what disease or condition a person has based on their signs and symptoms. Diagnostic tests may also be used to help plan treatment, find out how well treatment is working, and make a prognosis. There are many different types of diagnostic tests, examples include: • laboratory tests (such as blood and urine tests), • imaging tests (such as mammography and CT scan), • endoscopy (such as colonoscopy and bronchoscopy), and • biopsy.

Term		Definition
Diagnostic Trial		A research study that evaluates methods of detecting disease.
Differentiation		In cancer, this describes how much or how little tumour tissue looks like the normal tissue that it came from. Well-differentiated cancer cells look more like normal cells and tend to grow and spread more slowly than poorly differentiated or undifferentiated cancer cells. Differentiation is used in tumour grading systems, which are different for each type of cancer.
Digital Health Technology		The application of organised knowledge and skills in the form of devices, medicines, vaccines, procedures, and systems developed to solve a health problem and improve the quality of life.
Diploid		A term that refers to the presence of two complete sets of chromosomes in an organism's cells, with each parent contributing a chromosome to each pair. Humans are diploid, and most of the body's cells contain 23 chromosome pairs.
Disease-causing Mutation		See Predisposing Mutation.
Disease Free Survival	DFS	The proportion of patients for which no sign of cancer is found for a certain period after trial entry.
Dissemination		Communicating the findings of a research project to people who might find it useful.

Term		Definition
Diversity		Having people with different physical, social, and personal traits or characteristics in a group or organisation. These characteristics may include race, ethnicity, age, gender, sexual identity, religion, physical and mental ability, language, income, and education. Diversity may also include different life experiences, cultural backgrounds, beliefs, and interests in a group. In cancer research, efforts are being made to increase the diversity of people enrolled in clinical trials so that the trial results represent a wider group of people who would most likely benefit from the treatment or intervention being studied.
DNA Replication		The process by which the genome's DNA is copied in cells. Before a cell divides, it must first copy (or replicate) its entire genome so that each resulting daughter cell ends up with its own complete genome.
DNA Sequencing		The general laboratory technique for determining the exact sequence of nucleotides, or bases, in a DNA molecule. The sequence of the bases encodes the biological information that cells use to develop and operate. Establishing the sequence of DNA is key to understanding the function of genes and other parts of the genome. There are now several different methods available for DNA sequencing, each with its own characteristics, and the development of additional methods represents an active area of genomics research.

Term		Definition
Dose-dense Chemotherapy		A chemotherapy treatment plan in which drugs are given with less time between treatments than in a standard chemotherapy treatment plan.
Dose-dependent		Refers to the effects of treatment with a drug. If the effects change when the dose of the drug is changed, the effects are said to be dose-dependent.
Dose-escalation Study		A study that determines the best dose of a new drug or treatment. In a dose-escalation study, the dose of the test drug is increased a little at a time in different groups of people until the highest dose that does not cause harmful side effects is found. A dose-escalation study may also measure ways that the drug is used by the body and is often done as part of a phase I clinical trial. These trials usually include a small number of patients and may include healthy volunteers.
Dose-expansion Trials		Dose-expansion trials are clinical trials that evaluate the safety, pharmacokinetics, pharmacodynamics, and clinical activity of a new drug or treatment in a larger group of patients than in the initial dose-escalation trial.
Dose-limiting		Describes side effects of a drug or other treatment that are serious enough to prevent an increase in dose or level of that treatment.
Dosing Discontinuation		The point when a trial participant permanently stops taking the study drug. This may be at the end of the study, or before the end if the participant wants to stop taking the medicine for any reason.

Term		Definition
Double Blind		A trial where both the investigators and trial participants do not know which treatment is being given.
Double Helix		A pair of parallel helices intertwined about a common axis, especially that in the structure of the DNA molecule.
Downstaging		In cancer, changing the stage used to describe the extent of cancer in the body from a higher stage (indicating more extensive disease) to a lower stage (indicating less extensive disease). Staging is usually based on the size of the tumour and whether the cancer has spread. Downstaging may occur as a result of treatment that shrinks a tumour so it can be removed by surgery that otherwise could not have been done.
Drug Accountability Ratio	DAR	A log of study drugs kept by an investigator running a clinical trial. It lists many things about each drug, including the drug name, lot number, expiration date, the amount of drug received, used, returned, or thrown away, and the amount left. DARs help make sure that a clinical trial is carried out safely and correctly.
Drug Development		The process of bringing a new drug to market.
Drug Development Unit	DDU	A group specialising in drug development.

Term		Definition
Drug Resistance		When cancer cells or microorganisms, such as bacteria or viruses, do not respond to a drug that is usually able to kill or weaken them. Drug resistance may be present before treatment is given or may occur during or after treatment with the drug. In cancer treatment, there are many things that may cause resistance to anti-cancer drugs. For example, DNA changes or other genetic changes may alter the way the drug gets into the cancer cells or the way the drug is broken down within the cancer cells. Drug resistance can lead to cancer treatment not working or to the cancer coming back.

E

Term		Definition
Early Career Researchers	ECR	Researchers in the first four years (full-time equivalent) of their research activity, including the period of research training.
Echocardiogram		A scan used to look at the heart and nearby blood vessels. It is a type of ultrasound scan, which means a small probe is used to send out high-frequency sound waves that create echoes when they bounce off different parts of the body.
Effectiveness		How well a trial treatment works under 'real-world' conditions.
Efficacy		How well a trial treatment works under an ideal and controlled setting.
Electrocardiogram	ECG	An electrocardiogram is a test to record the electrical signals in the heart. It shows how the heart is beating.
Electromagnetic Radiation	EMR	Radiation that has both electric and magnetic fields and travels in waves. EMR can vary in strength from low energy to high energy. It comes from both natural and man-made sources and includes radio waves, microwaves, infrared light, visible light, ultraviolet light, x-rays, and gamma rays.
Electronic Data Capture	EDC	The collection of data using an electronic system rather than paper Case Report Forms (CRFs).
Electrophoresis		A laboratory technique used to separate DNA, RNA or protein molecules based on their size and electrical charge. An electric current is used to move the molecules through a gel or other matrix. Pores in the gel or matrix work like a sieve, allowing smaller molecules to move faster than larger molecules. To determine the size of the molecules in a sample, standards of known sizes are separated on the same gel and then compared to the sample.

Term		Definition
Electroporation Therapy	EPT	Treatment that generates electrical pulses through an electrode placed in a tumour to enhance the ability of anti-cancer drugs to enter tumour cells.
Eligibility Criteria		Requirements that patients must meet to take part in a particular clinical trial. For example, a trial might only accept participants who are above certain ages.
End-of-life Care		Care given to people who are near the end of life and have stopped treatment to cure or control their disease. End-of-life care includes physical, emotional, social, and spiritual support for patients and their families. The goal of end-of-life care is to control pain and other symptoms so the patient can be as comfortable as possible. End-of-life care may include palliative care, supportive care, and hospice care.
End of Treatment	EOT	A clinical trial finishes when the period of giving people different treatments to test them comes to an end. After the clinical trial has finished, there is a follow-up period of time, where people who were on the trial continue to be monitored to see how they do.
Endothermic		A reaction or process accompanied by or requiring the absorption of heat.
Endpoint		The results measured at the end of a study to see whether the research question was answered.

Term		Definition
Endpoint Adjudication Committee	EAC	Where endpoints in clinical studies are complex to assess and/or include subjective components or the study cannot be blinded, an EAC might be set up to harmonise and standardise endpoint assessment and to determine whether the endpoints meet protocol-specified criteria. In order to allow for an unbiased endpoint assessment the members of such a committee should be blinded to treatment assignment. Endpoint Adjudication Committees are, for example, widely used in the assessment of radiological endpoints. An EAC consists of clinical experts in a specific clinical area.
End-stage Cancer		See Terminal Cancer.
Enrolment		A participant's entry into a clinical trial. The same term may also be used to refer to the number of participants in a clinical trial.
Epidemiological Research		See Population Research.
Epigenetics		A field of study focused on changes in DNA that do not involve alterations to the underlying sequence. The DNA letters and the proteins that interact with DNA can have chemical modifications that change the degrees to which genes are turned on and off. Certain epigenetic modifications may be passed on from parent cell to daughter cell during cell division or from one generation to the next. The collection of all epigenetic changes in a genome is called an epigenome.
Epithelial		The cells that line the internal and external surfaces of the body.
Epitope		A part of a molecule that an antibody will recognise and bind to.

Term		Definition
Equality, Diversity and Inclusion	EDI	The aim to prevent discrimination on the basis of an individual or group of individuals' protected characteristics. Its goal is to give fair treatment and opportunity for all.
Equipoise		Where it is believed to be equally likely that either of the two treatment options is better.
Erythrocyte		See Red Blood Cell.
Essential Documents	EDs	The essential documents relating to a clinical trial are: • those which enable both the conduct of the clinical trial and the quality of the data produced to be evaluated, and • show whether the trial is, or has been, conducted in accordance with the applicable regulatory requirements.
Aetiology		The cause or origin of the disease.
European Economic Area	EEA	The EEA includes EU countries and also Iceland, Liechtenstein and Norway. It allows them to be part of the EU's single market.
European Medicines Agency	EMA	An agency of the European Union that oversees the use of medicinal products.
European Organisation for Research and Treatment of Cancer	EORTC	A European non-profit cancer research organisation.
Event-free Survival	EFS	The time after trial entry that a group of people in a clinical trial have not had their cancer come back or get worse.
Evidence-Based Medicine	EBM	The best scientific research available about a disease or health problem. This is used to make decisions about the best treatment to give.
Excision		See Resection.

Term		Definition
Exclusion Criteria		Requirements that set out who cannot take part in a clinical study. For example, people with a certain medical condition which may make it dangerous for them to take part.
Exogenous		Having an external cause or origin.
Expectant Management		Closely watching a patient's condition but not giving treatment unless symptoms appear or change, or there are changes in test results. Expectant management avoids problems that may be caused by treatments such as radiation or surgery. It is used to find early signs that the condition is getting worse. During expectant management, patients may be given certain exams and tests.
Experimental Group		The group in a clinical research study that receives the drug, vaccine, or other intervention being tested. Interventions may also include medical procedures (such as radiation therapy and surgery), medical devices, behaviour changes (such as diet and exercise), education programs, and counselling. Also called the intervention group and investigational group.
Experts by Experience		People who are experts through their experience of a particular illness or disability and services.
Explanatory Trial		A trial that measures the benefit of a treatment under ideal and controlled conditions.
External Agreement		An agreement between an organisation and relevant external parties, for example between an organisation and a research organisation. External agreements may be required to confirm issues such as indemnity, intellectual property, roles and responsibilities, data protection, confidentiality, financial and termination issues, standards of service and, where applicable, regulatory obligations.

Term		Definition
External Beam Radiation Therapy	EBRT	A form of radiotherapy that utilises a high-energy collimated beam of ionising radiation, from a source outside the body, to target and kill cancer cells.
Extracellular Fluid	ECF	Extracellular fluid surrounds all cells in the body. Extracellular fluid has two primary constituents: • the fluid component of the blood (plasma), and • the interstitial fluid (IF) that surrounds those cells not in the blood.
Ex Vivo		Latin *Outside of the living body*. Refers to a medical procedure in which an organ, cells, or tissue are taken from a living body for a treatment or procedure, and then returned to the living body.

F

Term		Definition
Factorial Design		A clinical trial design in which groups of participants receive one of several combinations of interventions. For example, a two-by-two factorial design involves four groups of participants. Each group receives one of the following pairs of interventions: • drug A and drug B, or • drug A and a placebo, or • drug B and a placebo, or • a placebo and a placebo. During the trial, all possible combinations of the two drugs (A and B and the placebos) are given to different groups of participants.
False Negative		A false negative is a test result which wrongly indicates that a given condition does not exist when it does.
False Positive		A false positive is a test result that wrongly indicates that a given condition exists when it does not.
Familial Cancer		Cancer that occurs in families more often than would be expected by chance. These cancers often occur at an early age and may indicate the presence of a gene mutation that increases the risk of cancer. They may also be a sign of shared environmental or lifestyle factors.

Term		Definition
Family Cancer Syndrome		A type of inherited disorder in which there is a higher-than-normal risk of certain types of cancer. Family cancer syndromes are caused by mutations (changes) in certain genes passed from parents to children. In a family cancer syndrome, certain patterns of cancer may be seen within families. These patterns include having several close family members (such as a mother, daughter, and sister) with the same type of cancer, developing cancer at an early age, or having two or more types of cancer develop in the same person. Examples of family cancer syndromes are hereditary breast and ovarian cancer syndrome. Also called hereditary cancer syndrome and inherited cancer syndrome.
Feasibility Study		Research done before a main study to answer the question 'Can the main study be carried out?' They aim to find out things such as whether patients and doctors are happy to take part, or how long it might take to collect the data.
Fine-needle Aspiration Biopsy		The removal of fluid, cells, or tissue with a thin needle for examination under a microscope.
'First-in-Human' Study	FIH	A type of clinical trial in which a new drug, procedure, or treatment is tested in humans for the first time. FIH studies take place after the new treatment has been tested in laboratory and animal studies and are usually carried out as phase I clinical trials.
First-Line Therapy		The first treatment given for a disease. It is often part of a standard set of treatments, such as surgery followed by chemotherapy and radiation. When used by itself, first-line therapy is the one accepted as the best treatment. If it does not cure the disease or it causes severe side effects, other treatments may be added or used instead. Also called induction therapy, primary therapy, and primary treatment.

Term		Definition
Five-year Survival Rate		The percentage of people in a study or treatment group who are alive five years after they were diagnosed with or started treatment for a disease, such as cancer. The disease may or may not have come back.
Fluorescence In Situ Hybridisation	FISH	A laboratory technique used to detect and locate a specific DNA sequence on a chromosome.
Fluoroscopy		An x-ray procedure that makes it possible to see internal organs in motion.
Focus Group		A small group of people brought together to talk. The purpose is to listen and gather information. It is a good way to find out how people feel or think about an issue, or to come up with possible solutions to problems.
Follow-up (Care)		Where further data is obtained relating to a trial participant after active treatment over a specified amount of time. Follow-up care can check a patient's recovery, monitor for any new problems and suggest further tests and/or treatment.
Food and Drug Administration	FDA	The competent authority for the regulation of food and drugs in the United States of America.

Term		Definition
Formalin Fixed Paraffin Embedded (Tumour Blocks)	FFPE	A way of processing tissue that has been taken from a suspected tumour. Most fresh tissue is very easily damaged and thus impossible to cut into thin sections for examination under a microscope. The tissue needs to be chemically preserved or 'fixed' (in formalin in this case) and supported in some way whilst it is being cut. If the tissue is embedded in liquid paraffin which then sets, a paraffin block is formed, which will then allow thin sections to be cut from it (paraffin sections). Patients taking part in trials are often asked by researchers if they are willing to donate tumour blocks made during their diagnosis for either research associated with the trial or for future research – these are usually FFPE blocks.
Frameshift Mutation		The insertion or deletion of nucleotide bases in numbers that are not multiples of three.
Free Radical		A type of unstable molecule that is made during normal cell metabolism (chemical changes that take place in a cell). Free radicals can build up in cells and cause damage to other molecules, such as DNA, lipids, and proteins. This damage may increase the risk of cancer and other diseases.
Free Radical Scavenger		A substance, such as an antioxidant, that helps protect cells from the damage caused by free radicals.
Full Blood Count	FBC	A measure of the number of red blood cells, white blood cells, and platelets in the blood. The amount of haemoglobin (a substance in the blood that carries oxygen) and haematocrit (the amount of whole blood that is made up of red blood cells) are also measured. A full blood count is used to help diagnose and monitor many conditions.
Funder		The organisation providing funding for running the clinical trial.

Term		Definition
Fusion Biopsy		A biopsy procedure that combines the pictures from an MRI scan and an ultrasound to create a detailed 3-D image.
		This procedure makes it easier to see an abnormal area of tissue in order to guide the biopsy needle into the abnormal area. A sample of tissue can then be removed and checked under a microscope for signs of cancer.
		A fusion biopsy may help find cancer cells that may be missed with other types of biopsies. It may help find cancer at an early stage and plan cancer treatment.
		Also called MRI ultrasound fusion-guided biopsy.

G

Term		Definition
Gamma Knife Therapy		A treatment using gamma rays, a type of high-energy radiation that can be tightly focused on small tumours or other lesions in the head or neck, so very little normal tissue receives radiation. The gamma rays are aimed at the tumour from many different angles at once and deliver a large dose of radiation exactly to the tumour in one treatment session. This procedure is a type of stereotactic radiosurgery. Gamma Knife therapy is not a knife and is not surgery (Gamma Knife is a registered trademark of Elekta Instruments, Inc.).
Gamma Radiation		A type of high-energy radiation that is different to X-rays.
Gene		The functional and physical unit of heredity passed from parent to offspring. Genes are pieces of DNA, and most genes contain the information for making a specific protein.
Gene Amplification		An increase in the number of copies of a gene in a genome. Cancer cells, for example, sometimes produce multiple copies of a gene in response to signals from other cells or the environment.
Gene Expression		The process by which the information encoded in a gene is used to either make RNA molecules that code for proteins or to make non-coding RNA molecules that serve other functions.
Gene Mapping		The process of determining the location of genes on chromosomes.
Gene Pool		The combination of all the genes (including alleles) present in a reproducing population or species.
General Data Protection Regulation	GDPR	The rules around the use of personal data. In the UK this is covered by the Data Protection Act 2018.
Generalisability		How well the trial findings can be applied to other patients and settings?

Term		Definition
Gene Regulation		The process used to control the timing, location and amount in which genes are expressed. The process can be complicated and is carried out by a variety of mechanisms, including through regulatory proteins and chemical modification of DNA. Gene regulation is key to the ability of an organism to respond to environmental changes.
Gene Therapy		A medical technology that aims to produce a therapeutic effect through the manipulation of gene expression or through altering the biological properties of living cells.
Gene Therapy Advisory Committee	GTAC	The national ethics committee for clinical trials involving medicinal products for gene therapy.
Genetic Code		The instructions contained in a gene that tell a cell how to make a specific protein. Each gene's code uses the four nucleotide bases of DNA (adenine, cytosine, guanine and thymine) in various ways to spell out three-letter 'codons' that specify which amino acid is needed at each position within a protein.
Genetic Engineering		A process that uses laboratory-based technologies to alter the DNA makeup of an organism.
Genetic Profile		Information about changes in specific genes, gene expression, or chromosomes in cells or tissue of a person. These changes may be a sign of a disease or condition, such as cancer. They may also be a sign that a person has an increased risk of developing a specific disease or condition or of having a child or other family member with the disease or condition. A genetic profile may be used to help diagnose disease, plan treatment, or find out how well treatment is working.
Geneticist		A scientist who has special training in the study of genes and heredity (the passing of genetic information from parents to their children). A medical geneticist is a doctor who specialises in diagnosing and treating genetic disorders or conditions. Medical geneticists also counsel individuals and families at risk for certain genetic disorders or cancers.

Term		Definition
Genetics		The study of genes, genetic variation, and heredity in organisms.
Genetic Testing		Genetic testing looks for changes (mutations or variants) in your DNA. Genetic testing is useful in many areas of medicine and can change the medical care you or your family member receives. For example, genetic testing can provide a diagnosis for a genetic condition such as information about the risk of developing cancer.
Genome		A genome is all the genetic information of an organism consisting of nucleotide sequences of DNA.
Genome Characterisation		A laboratory method that uses a sample of tissue, blood, or other body fluid to learn about all the genes in a person or in a specific cell type, and the way those genes interact with each other and with the environment. Genomic characterisation may be carried out to find out why some people get certain diseases whilst others do not. Genomic characterisation may also be carried out on tumour tissue to look for mutations or other genetic changes in a tumour's DNA. This may help doctors understand how different types of cancer form and respond to treatment, which may lead to new ways to diagnose, treat, and prevent cancer. Also called genomic profiling.
Genome-wide Association Study	GWAS	A study that compares DNA markers across the genome (the complete genetic material in a person) in people with a disease or trait to people without the disease or trait. These studies may uncover clues to help prevent, diagnose, and treat disease.
Genomic Profiling		See Genome Characterisation.
Genomics		An interdisciplinary field of biology focusing on the structure, function, evolution, mapping, and editing of genomes.

Term		Definition
Genomic Sequencing		A laboratory method that is used to determine the entire genetic makeup of a specific organism or cell type. This method can be used to find changes in areas of the genome. These changes may help scientists understand how specific diseases, such as cancer, form. Results of genomic sequencing may also be used to diagnose and treat disease.
Genomic Variation		DNA sequence differences among individuals or populations. Some variants influence biological function (such as a mutation that causes a genetic disease), whilst others have no biological effects.
Genotoxicity		The property of chemical agents that damage the genetic information within a cell, causing mutations, which may lead to cancer.
Genotyping		The process of determining differences in the genetic makeup of an individual by examining the individual's DNA sequence using biological assays and comparing it to another individual's sequence or a reference sequence.
Gold Fiducial Markers		See Gold Seeds.
Gold Fiducial Marker Seeds		See Gold Seeds.
Gold-seed Fiducial Markers		See Gold Seeds.
Gold Seeds		Tiny, gold seeds, about the size of a grain of rice, that are put in and/or around a tumour to show exactly where it is in the body. Doctors are then able to target the tumour directly and give higher doses of radiation with less harm to nearby healthy tissue. Also called gold fiducial markers, gold fiducial marker seeds, and gold-seed fiducial markers.

Term		Definition
Gold Standard		The method, procedure, or measurement that is widely accepted as being the best available. New developments should be compared against the gold standard.
Good Clinical Practice	GCP	A set of internationally recognised standards which must be followed during all aspects of clinical trials involving human participants.
Good Manufacturi ng Practice	GMO	That part of quality assurance which ensures that medicinal products are consistently produced and controlled to the quality standards appropriate to their intended use and as required by the marketing authorisation (MA) or product specification.
Governance Agreements for Research Ethics Committees	GAfREC	A policy document written by the UK Health Department describing what is expected from the research ethics committees that review research proposals relating to areas of the UK Health Department's responsibility. It also explains when review by these committees is required.
Grade		See Tumour Grade.
Guanine		One of the four nucleotide bases in DNA, with the other three being adenine (A), cytosine (C) and thymine (T). Within a double-stranded DNA molecule, guanine bases on one strand pair with cytosine bases on the opposite strand. The sequence of the four nucleotide bases encodes DNA's information.

H

Term		Definition
Haemoglobin		A red protein responsible for transporting oxygen in the blood.
Health Disparity		A type of preventable health difference that is closely linked with social, political, economic, and environmental disadvantage. Health disparities may occur because of race, ethnicity, sex, gender identity, sexual orientation, age, religion, disability, education, income, where people live, or other characteristics. For example, certain race and ethnic groups may have higher rates of disease, disability, and death than those in other groups because they are more likely to have problems having access to good health care, healthy food, or the latest medical treatments.
Health Economics	HE	A study of the cost-effectiveness of a healthcare treatment or service.
Health Equity		A situation in which all people are given the chance to live as healthy a life as possible regardless of their race, ethnicity, sex, gender identity, sexual orientation, disability, education, job, religion, language, where they live, or other factors. A lack of health equity can result in differences in health outcomes, such as rates and severity of disease, disability, death, and quality of life.
Health History		See Medical History.
Health Research Authority	HRA	An NHS organisation established to protect and promote the interests of patients and the public in health research. The National Research Ethics Service (NRES) is now part of the HRA.

Term		Definition
Helical Computed Tomography	HCT	A procedure that uses a computer linked to an x-ray machine to make a series of detailed pictures of areas inside the body. The x-ray machine scans the body in a spiral path. This allows more images to be made in a shorter time than with older CT methods. A dye may be injected into a vein or swallowed to help the organs or tissues show up more clearly on the x-ray. HCT creates more detailed pictures and may be better at finding small abnormal areas inside the body. It may be used to help diagnose disease, plan treatment, or find out how well treatment is working. Also called a spiral CT scan.
Helical Tomotherapy		See Tomotherapy.
Hereditary Cancer Syndrome		See Family Cancer Syndrome.
Heritable cancers		Cancer itself cannot be passed down from parents to children, and genetic changes in tumour cells cannot be passed down either. However, a genetic change that increases the risk of cancer can be passed down (inherited) if it is present in a parent's egg or sperm cells. Cancer cells are defined by two heritable properties. They and their progeny: • reproduce in defiance of the normal restraints on cell division, and • invade and colonise territories normally reserved for other cells.

Term		Definition
Heterozygous		Heterozygous, as related to genetics, refers to having inherited different versions (alleles) of a genomic marker from each biological parent. Thus, an individual who is heterozygous for a genomic marker has two different versions of that marker. By contrast, an individual who is homozygous for a marker has identical versions of that marker.
High Dose-rate Remote Radiation Therapy		A type of internal radiation treatment in which the radioactive source is removed between treatments.
High-Energy Photon Therapy		A type of radiation therapy that uses high-energy photons (units of light energy). High-energy photons penetrate deeply into tissues to reach tumours whilst giving less radiation to superficial tissues such as the skin.
High-Intensity Focused Ultrasound	HIFU	A non-invasive therapeutic technique that uses non-ionising ultrasonic waves to heat or ablate tissue.
Histochemistry		See Histology.
Histologic Grade		See Tumour Grade.
Histone		A protein that provides structural support for a chromosome.
Histology		The microscopic study of tissues and organs through sectioning, staining, and examining those sections under a microscope. Histology allows for the visualisation of tissue structure and characteristic changes the tissue may have undergone. Also called microscopic anatomy or histochemistry,
Histopathology		The study of diseased cells and tissues using a microscope.
Historic Cohort Study		A research study in which the medical records of groups of individuals who are alike in many ways but differ by a certain characteristic (for example, female nurses who smoke and those who do not

Term		Definition
		smoke) are compared for a particular outcome (such as lung cancer). Also called a retrospective cohort study.
Homogeneity		The quality or state of being all the same or all of the same kind.
Homozygous		Homozygous, as related to genetics, refers to having inherited the same versions (alleles) of a genomic marker from each biological parent. Thus, an individual who is homozygous for a genomic marker has two identical versions of that marker. By contrast, an individual who is heterozygous for a marker has two different versions of that marker.
Hormone Therapy		Treatment that removes, blocks, or adds hormones to destroy or slow the growth of cancer cells. Also called hormonal therapy or endocrine therapy.
Hot Nodule		When radioactive material is used to examine the thyroid with a scanner, nodules that collect more radioactive material than the surrounding thyroid tissue are considered 'hot.' Hot nodules are sometimes called hyperfunctioning nodules. Hot nodules are rarely malignant.
Hotspot		In genetics, an area of DNA that is likely to mutate (change).
Hot Tumour		Describes a tumour that is likely to trigger a strong immune response. Hot tumours often have many molecules on their surface that allow T-cells (a type of immune cell) to attack and kill the tumour cells. Hot tumours usually respond to immunotherapy. Melanoma, non-small cell lung cancer, and cancers of the bladder, head and neck, kidney, and liver are usually considered hot tumours.

Term		Definition
Human Genome Project		A large international collaborative effort that mapped and sequenced the human genome for the first time. Conducted from 1990 to 2003, the project was historic in its scope and scale as well as its ground-breaking approach for the free release of genomic data well ahead of publication, leading to a new ethos for data sharing in biomedical research.
Human Genome Reference Sequence		An accepted representation of the human genome sequence that is used by researchers as a standard for comparison to DNA sequences generated in their studies.
Human Papillomavirus	HPV	A viral infection that commonly causes skin or mucous membrane growths (warts). There are more than 100 varieties of human papillomavirus.
Human Pharmacology		Human pharmacology represents the first stage of testing in human participants, 'first-in-human' studies. Although the treatment will have been thoroughly tested in laboratory and animal studies, side effects in participants cannot be completely known ahead of time.
Human Tissue Authority	HTA	An organisation that ensures human tissue samples are used safely and ethically and with proper consent. It regulates organisations that remove, store, and use tissue for research, medical treatment, post-mortem examination, teaching and display in public.
Hybrid Image		The fusion of two or more imaging technologies into a single, new form of imaging. Typically, this new form is synergistic i.e., more powerful than the sum of its parts.
Hyper-fractionated Radiation Therapy		See Super-fractionated Radiation Therapy.

Term		Definition
Hyperplasia		An increase in the number of cells in an organ or tissue. These cells appear normal under a microscope. They are not cancer but may become cancerous.
Hyperthermia Treatment		A type of medical treatment in which body tissue is exposed to temperatures above body temperature, in the region of 40-45 °C.
Hypo-fractionation		A treatment schedule in which the total dose of radiation is divided into large doses and treatments are given once a day or less often.
Hypokalaemia		A metabolic imbalance characterised by extremely low potassium levels in the blood.
Hypothesis		A statement that predicts the expected outcome of a study. This is made on the basis of current available evidence. In a trial, this would be proven or disproven based on the data collected.

I

Term		Definition
Idiopathic		Describes a disease of unknown cause.
Image Guided Radiotherapy	IGRT	A type of radiation therapy that uses powerful energy beams to kill cancer. The energy can come from X-rays, protons or other sources. In IGRT, images are used to help plan the treatment.
Imaging		A procedure that creates pictures of internal body parts, tissues, or organs to make a diagnosis. The images are used to plan treatment, find out whether treatment is working, or observe a disease over time.
Imaging Modality		The term used for different types of imaging procedures and therapies.
Imaging Procedure		A test that takes detailed pictures of areas inside the body. Examples of imaging procedures are computed tomography (CT), mammography, ultrasonography, magnetic resonance imaging (MRI), and nuclear medicine tests. Imaging procedures use different forms of energy, such as X-rays (high-energy radiation), ultrasound (high-energy sound waves), radio waves, and radioactive substances. They may be used to help diagnose disease, plan treatment, or find out how well treatment is working. Also called an imaging test.
Imaging Test		See Imaging Procedure.
Immune Adjuvant		A drug that stimulates the immune system to respond to disease.

Term		Definition
Immune Cell		A cell that is part of the immune system and helps the body fight infections and other diseases.
		Immune cells develop from stem cells in the bone marrow and become different types of white blood cells. These include neutrophils, eosinophils, basophils, mast cells, monocytes, macrophages, dendritic cells, natural killer cells, and lymphocytes (B-cells and T-cells).
Immune Response		The way the body defends itself against substances it sees as harmful or foreign.
		In an immune response, the immune system recognises the antigens (usually proteins) on the surface of substances or microorganisms, such as bacteria or viruses, and attacks and destroys, or tries to destroy them.
		Cancer cells also have antigens on their surface. Sometimes, the immune system sees these antigens as foreign and mounts an immune response against them. This helps the body fight cancer.
Immune System		A complex network of organs, cells and proteins that defends the body against infection, whilst protecting the body's own cells.
		The immune system keeps a record of every germ (microbe) it has ever defeated so it can recognise and destroy the microbe quickly if it enters the body again.

Term		Definition
Immunity		Being resistant to a particular infectious disease or pathogen. Humans have three types of immunity: • Everyone is born with innate (or natural) immunity, a type of general protection. • Adaptive (or active) immunity develops throughout our lives. Adaptive immunity develops when humans are exposed to diseases or through immunisation with vaccines. • Passive immunity is 'borrowed' from another source and it lasts for a short time. Humans can get passive immunity through antibody-containing blood products such as immune globulin, which may be given when immediate protection from a specific disease is needed.
Immunosuppressive Medicine		Drugs or medicines that lower the body's ability to reject a transplanted organ.
Immunosuppressive Therapy		Treatment that lowers the activity of the body's immune system. This reduces its ability to fight infections and other diseases, such as cancer. Immunosuppressive therapy may be used to keep a person from rejecting a bone marrow or organ transplant. It may also be used to treat conditions in which the immune system is overactive, such as autoimmune diseases and allergies. Some types of immunosuppressive therapy may increase a person's risk of cancer by lowering the body's ability to kill cancer cells.
Immunotherapy		See biotherapy.

Term		Definition
Impaired Hepatic Function		Hepatic impairment is when the liver stops working properly and cannot perform its basic functions.
Incapacitated Adult		An adult unable by virtue of physical or mental incapacity to give informed consent.
Incidence		The number of events of a certain outcome in a population during a given period of time.
Inclusion Criteria		Requirements that set out who can take part in a clinical study, for example, people within a certain age range.
Incomplete Penetrance		A term that describes when some people with a disease-causing mutation (change) in a gene develop the disease whilst others do not. For example, certain gene mutations cause cancer, but because of incomplete penetrance, not everyone who has the mutation will develop cancer. Currently, there is no way of knowing which people who have a cancer-causing gene mutation will develop cancer. Also called reduced penetrance.
Independent Data Monitoring Committee	IDMC	A group of independent experts who monitor the safety and scientific integrity of a clinical trial. The group can recommend to the Trial Steering Committee that a study be stopped or amended if it is not effective, is harming participants, or is unlikely to serve its aims.
Independent Variable		A variable in a study that is controlled by researchers. For example, the treatment given to a patient. The variable is independent of other variables recorded in the study.

Term		Definition
Indication		A disease, symptom, or set of circumstances that make a particular test, medication, procedure, or surgery advisable. For a treatment, an indication refers to the use of that treatment for a particular disease.
Induction Therapy		See first-line therapy.
Infiltrating Cancer		See Invasive Cancer.
Informed Consent		A process by which a patient learns about and understands the purpose, benefits and risks of participating in a trial and then voluntarily confirms if they want to take part. This includes reading and understanding the relevant patient information sheet (PIS).
Informed Consent Form	ICF	The document signed by the patient participant to confirm their agreement to take part in a trial.
Infrared Coagulation		A technique in which abnormal tissue is exposed to a burst of infrared light (a type of radiation). This causes blood in veins in the tissue to coagulate (harden) and the abnormal tissue to shrink.
Infrared Thermography		In medicine, a procedure in which an infrared camera (one that senses heat) is used to measure temperature differences on the surface of the body. The camera takes pictures that show areas of possible abnormal cell growth as abnormal tissue gives off more heat than normal tissue.

Term		Definition
Inherited Cancer Syndrome		See Family Cancer Syndrome.
In Situ		Refers to cancer that has not spread to nearby tissue, also called non-invasive cancer.
Inspection		The act by a competent authority of conducting an official review of documents, facilities, records, quality assurance arrangements, and any other resources that are deemed by the competent authority to be related to the clinical trial and that may be located at the site of the trial, at the sponsor's and/or contract research organisation's facilities, or at other establishments which the competent authority sees fit to inspect. In the UK, the MHRA's Good Clinical Practice (GCP) Inspectorate is part of the Inspection, Standards and Enforcement Division of the MHRA.
Institute of Cancer Research	ICR	One of the world's most influential cancer research organisations. The ICR is a UK charity and member institution of the University of London.
Institutional Review Board	IRB	The generic term used by the Food & Drugs Administration (FDA) in the United States for independent ethics committees that have been formally designated to review and monitor biomedical research involving human subjects.
Integrated Research Applications System	IRAS	The online application system used to apply for most permissions and approvals for research in health and social care in the UK.
Integrative Medicine		A combination of medical treatments to help manage symptoms and side effects.

Term		Definition
Intellectual Property	IP	The novel or previously undescribed tangible output of any intellectual activity. It has an owner and can be bought, sold or licensed and must be adequately protected. It can include inventions, industrial processes, software, data, written works, designs and images.
Intensification Therapy		Treatment that is given after cancer has disappeared following the initial therapy. Intensification therapy is used to kill any cancer cells that may be left in the body. It may include radiation therapy, a stem cell transplant, or treatment with drugs that kill cancer cells. Also called consolidation therapy and post-remission therapy.
Intensity-Modulated Radiotherapy	IMRT	Intensity-modulated radiation therapy is an advanced type of radiation therapy that uses powerful energy beams to kill cancer cells. The energy can come from X-rays, protons or other sources.
Intensive Chemotherapy		Treatment that uses anti-cancer drugs given at high doses or over several months to try to cure cancer or cause remission. Intensive chemotherapy is used to treat certain types of cancer, including leukaemia and lymphoma, and may be given with other therapy before a bone marrow or stem cell transplant. It can lower the number of normal blood-forming cells in the bone marrow and can cause other severe side effects, so it is usually given in a hospital.

Term		Definition
Intention to Treat		Where all trial participants are included in the statistical analysis according to the treatment they were originally assigned regardless of what treatment (if any) they received.
Interaction		Where the effect of one independent variable on the outcome is affected by the value of a second independent variable. For example, when the effect of an experimental statin on blood cholesterol is influenced by the age of the trial participant.
Interactive Response Technology	IRT	IRT is software that enables activities such as randomisation into clinical trials and dispensing medications in a blinded trial. Examples include telephone-based Interactive Voice Response Systems (IVRS) or internet-based, Interactive Web Response Systems (IWRS). These technologies are also used in other trial management activities.
Intercellular Communication		The transfer of information from one cell to another. Cells signal each other by direct contact with each other or by the release of a substance from one cell that is taken up by another cell. Intercellular communication is important for cells to grow and work normally. Cells that lose the ability to respond to signals from other cells may become cancer cells. Also called cell-cell signalling and cell-to-cell signalling.

Term		Definition
Interim Analysis		An analysis of the current available data from an ongoing trial. This can be used to inform decisions about whether or not the trial should continue. The timing and frequency of interim analyses should be specified in the protocol.
Internal Agreements		An agreement between an organisation and relevant internal parties. Examples include: • agreements, memoranda or documentation between an ' R&D Office' and clinical and non-clinical support services in order to facilitate engagement and internal authorisation from named support service leads, • agreements between a principal investigator/chief investigator and support service or stakeholders within an organisation, • agreements between the organisation and relevant party for resources who require an honorary research contract or letter of access. These agreements may be in the form of a standardised document or email format.
Internal Beam Radiotherapy	IBR	IBR kills cancer cells with a high dose of radiation through an implant inside the body. The implant directs energy directly at the tumour, thus helping spare nearby tissues and reducing side effects.
Internal Radiation Therapy		See Brachytherapy.

Term		Definition
International Conference on Harmonisation	ICH	The ICH is a joint initiative involving both regulators and research-based industry focusing on the technical requirements for medicinal products containing new drugs to establish common standards for clinical trials. Its objectives are: • To improve the efficiency of new drug development and registration processes, and • To promote public health, prevent duplication of clinical trials in humans and minimise the use of animal testing without compromising safety and effectiveness
International Recognition Procedure	IRP	The UK's International Recognition Procedure was applied from 1 January 2024 for the purpose of accelerating the approval of new medicinal products, by allowing medicinal products approved in other countries to be fast-tracked for marketing authorisation in the UK, whilst retaining oversight and control (see accelerated approval).
International Standard Randomised Controlled Trial Number	ISRCTN	A simple numeric system for the unique identification of randomised controlled trials worldwide. The randomly generated number is unique to a registered trial, thereby ensuring that the trial can be simply and unambiguously tracked throughout its lifecycle. The ISRCTN Register also accepts registration of other forms of studies designed to assess the efficacy of healthcare interventions.

Term		Definition
Interstitial Fluid		The body fluid between blood vessels and cells, containing nutrients from capillaries by diffusion and holding waste products discharged by cells due to metabolism.
Intervention		Any trial treatment, medical device, procedure or activity under investigation in the trial.
Interventional Trial		A trial where participants receive specific interventions (or no intervention) according to the research plan or protocol created by the investigators. These interventions may be medical products, such as drugs or devices, procedures, or changes to a participant's behaviour, for example, diet.
Intervention Group		See Experimental Group.
Intraoperative Radiation Therapy	IORT	Radiation treatment aimed directly at a tumour during surgery. IORT directs radiation to the target area whilst minimising the effect on the surrounding tissue. IORT is used to treat cancers that are difficult to remove during surgery and is used when there is a concern that tiny amounts of unseen cancer might remain.
Intraoperative Ultrasound		A procedure that uses ultrasound (high-energy sound waves that are bounced off internal tissues and organs) during surgery. Sonograms (pictures made by ultrasound) of the inside of the body are viewed on a computer to help a surgeon find tumours or other problems during the operation.

Term		Definition
Intravenous Pyelogram	IVP	An x-ray image of the kidneys, ureters, bladder, and prostate in men, that is taken after a contrast dye is injected into a vein. As the dye travels through the bloodstream, it collects in these organs, turning them bright white. This allows the radiologist to see blockages or other urinary tract problems on the x-ray pictures. An intravenous pyelogram may be used to help diagnose certain urinary tract conditions, such as kidney or bladder stones, kidney cysts, urinary tract tumours, and an enlarged prostate. Also called intravenous urogram.
Intravenous Urogram	IVU	See Intravenous Pyelogram.
Invasive Cancer		Cancer that has spread outside the layer of tissue where it started and has the potential to grow into other tissues or parts of the body. Also known as Infiltrating Cancer.
Investigational Group		See Experimental Group.
Investigational Medicinal Product	IMP	Medicinal products are substances that are used to prevent illness from occurring, treat disease or relieve symptoms. An IMP is a medicinal product being tested within a clinical trial or a substance used as a comparison e.g., a placebo within a trial.
Investigational Medicinal Product Dossier	IMPD	The IMPD includes summaries of information related to the quality, manufacture and control of any IMP (including reference product and placebo), and data from non-clinical and clinical studies.

Term		Definition
Investigational New Drug	IND	A substance that has been tested in the laboratory and has been approved for testing in people. Clinical trials test how well INDs work and whether they are safe to use. An IND may be approved for use in one disease or condition, but still be considered investigational in other diseases or conditions. Also called an experimental drug, investigational agent and investigational drug.
Investigator		A person who is conducting a clinical trial. The expert leading the overall research in multiple hospitals is referred to as the chief investigator and those responsible for the conduct of a trial at a specific hospital are principal investigators.
Investigator-Initiated Trials	IIT	Clinical trials which are developed and run by clinicians and researchers based at universities and the NHS rather than being led by pharmaceutical companies.
Investigator's Brochure	IB	A record of data available on the investigational medicinal product which are relevant to the study of the product in humans. This is maintained by a drug developer, manufacturer or investigator. It provides the reasons for key features of a protocol such as dose, methods of administration and safety monitoring.
Investigator Site File	ISF	The ISF contains all essential documents held by the principal investigator(s) conducting a trial which individually and collectively permit the evaluation of the conduct of a trial and the quality of the data produced.

Term		Definition
INVOLVE		A national advisory group which promotes and supports greater public involvement in the NHS, public health and social care research.
Ionising Radiation		Ionising radiation, including nuclear radiation, consists of subatomic particles or electromagnetic waves that have sufficient energy to ionise atoms or molecules by detaching electrons from them.
Irradiated		Treated with radiation.
Irradiation		The use of high-energy radiation from X-rays, gamma rays, neutrons, protons, and other sources to kill cancer cells and shrink tumours. Radiation may come from a machine outside the body (external beam radiation therapy), or it may come from radioactive material placed in the body near cancer cells (internal radiation therapy or brachytherapy). Systemic irradiation uses a radioactive substance, such as a radiolabelled monoclonal antibody, that travels in the blood to tissues throughout the body. Also called radiation therapy and radiotherapy.

J

Term		Definition
Janus Kinase 2 gene	JAK2 gene	A gene that makes a protein that sends signals in cells to promote cell growth and helps control the number of red blood cells, white blood cells, and platelets that are made in bone marrow. Mutated (altered) forms of the JAK gene have been found in some types of blood conditions. These changes may cause the body to make too many blood cells.
Jewett staging system		A staging system for prostate cancer that uses ABCD. • 'A' and 'B' refer to cancer that is confined to the prostate, • 'C' refers to cancer that has grown out of the prostate but has not spread to lymph nodes or other places in the body, • 'D' refers to cancer that has spread to lymph nodes or to other places in the body. Also called ABCD rating and Whitmore-Jewett staging system.
Joint Sponsor		Where two or more organisations share a significant interest in a study, they may elect to act as joint sponsors.

K

Term		Definition
Karnofsky Performance Status	KPS	A standard way of measuring the ability of cancer patients to perform ordinary tasks. KPS scores range from 0 to 100; a higher score means a patient is better able to perform daily activities. KPS can be used to determine a patient's prognosis, to measure relative changes in a patient's ability to function or to decide if a patient could be included in a clinical trial.
Karyotype		An individual's complete set of chromosomes.
Killer T-cell		A type of immune cell that can kill certain cells, including foreign cells, cancer cells, and cells infected with a virus. Killer T-cells can be separated from other blood cells, grown in the laboratory, and then given to a patient to kill cancer cells. A killer T-cell is a type of white blood cell and a type of lymphocyte. Also called cytotoxic T-cell and cytotoxic T-lymphocyte.

L

Term		Definition
Laser Interstitial Thermal Therapy	LITT	Laser interstitial thermal therapy uses a very narrow, focused beam of light to shrink or destroy cancer cells.
		It can be used to cut out tumours without damaging other tissue.
		Laser therapy is often given through a thin, lit tube that is put inside the body. Thin fibres at the end of the tube direct the light at the cancer cells.
Late Effects		Side effects of cancer treatment that may occur months or years after treatment has finished.
Late-stage Cancer		Cancer that is far along in its growth and has spread to the lymph nodes or other places in the body.
Lay		Non-professional.
Lay Person		In research, it refers to people who are neither researchers nor health care professionals.
Lay Summary		A summary of a research idea, protocol or explanation of results that can be easily understood by members of the public.
		It should be written in plain English, avoid the use of jargon and explain any technical terms that are used.
Legal Representative (in relation to informed consent of vulnerable subjects in CTIMPs)		A person who gives written informed consent on behalf of a vulnerable subject in a CTIMP as defined in Schedule 1, Part 1 (2) of The Medicines for Human Use (Clinical Trials) Regulations, as amended.
Legal Representative (in relation to sponsor role)		If the main sponsor of a clinical trial with a medicinal product is not based in the European Economic Area (EEA), for example, an American or Japanese company, it is a statutory requirement to appoint a legal representative based in the EEA for the purposes of the trial.

Term		Definition
Letters of Access		Letters of access enable NHS employees or staff with an honorary clinical contract (e.g. clinical academics) with one NHS organisation to conduct research in another NHS organisation.
Levels of Evidence		A ranking system used to describe the strength of the results measured in a clinical trial or research study. The design of the study (such as a case report for an individual patient or a randomised double-blinded controlled clinical trial) and the endpoints measured (such as survival or quality of life) affect the strength of the evidence.
Leukocyte		See White Blood Cell.
Lifetime Risk		A measure of the risk that a certain event will happen during a person's lifetime. In cancer research, it is usually given as the likelihood that a person who is free of a certain type of cancer will develop or die from that type of cancer during his or her lifetime.
Light-emitting Diode Therapy	LEDT	Treatment with drugs that become active and may kill cancer cells when exposed to light. LEDT is a type of photodynamic therapy, which uses a special type of light to activate the drug.
Linac		A machine that uses electricity to form a stream of fast-moving subatomic particles. This creates high-energy radiation that may be used to treat cancer. Also called linear accelerator, mega-voltage linear accelerator, and MeV linear accelerator.
Linear Accelerator		See Linac.

Term		Definition
Local Heterogeneity		When mutations (changes) in different genes cause the same disease or condition.
		Each mutation by itself is enough to cause the disease or condition. For example, xeroderma pigmentosum (a rare, inherited disorder with a very high risk of developing skin cancer and other types of cancer) is caused by having a mutation in one of at least nine different genes involved in repairing damaged DNA.
Localised Cancer		Cancer that is confined to the area where it started and has not spread to other parts of the body.
Localised Therapy		Treatment that is directed to a specific organ or limited area of the body, such as the breast or an abnormal growth on the skin. Examples of local therapy used in cancer are surgery, radiation therapy, cryotherapy, laser therapy, and topical therapy.
Locally Advanced Cancer		Cancer that has spread from where it started to nearby tissue or lymph nodes.
Locally Recurrent Cancer		Cancer that has recurred (come back) at or near the same place as the original (primary) tumour, usually after a period of time during which the cancer could not be detected.
Low-dose Chemotherapy		Treatment in which low doses of anti-cancer drugs are given on a continuous or frequent, regular schedule (such as daily or weekly), usually over a long time. Low-dose chemotherapy causes less severe side effects than standard chemotherapy. Giving low doses of chemotherapy may stop the growth of new blood vessels that tumours need to grow. Also called metronomic chemotherapy.

Term		Definition
Low-dose Computed Tomography (Scan)	LDCT	A procedure that uses a computer linked to an x-ray machine that gives off a very low dose of radiation to make a series of detailed pictures of areas inside the body. The pictures are taken from different angles and are used to create 3-D views of tissues and organs.
Low-dose Radiation Therapy	LDRT	Radiation treatment in which the total dose of radiation is less than that given in standard radiation therapy. In low-dose radiation therapy, the total dose may be given in fewer treatments or over a shorter period of time (fewer days or weeks) than standard radiation therapy. This may cause less damage to nearby healthy tissue.
Lymph		A clear-to-white fluid made of white blood cells, especially lymphocytes, the cells that attack bacteria in the blood and body tissues.
Lymph Gland		See Lymph Node.
Lymph Node		Lymph nodes are small lumps of tissue that contain white blood cells, which fight infection. They are part of the body's immune system. Also called the lymph gland.
Lymphocyte		A type of white blood cell in the immune system.
Lymph System		An organ system that is part of the immune system, and complementary to the circulatory system. It consists of a large network of lymphatic vessels, lymph nodes, lymphoid organs, lymphoid tissues and lymph.

M

Term		Definition
Machine Learning		A field of computer science that develops the processes by which computers are taught how to learn and perform certain functions without being specifically programmed to perform those functions. Machine learning involves analysing very large amounts of information to improve a computer's ability to make decisions or predictions. Machine learning is an element of artificial intelligence (AI). In medicine, the use of machine learning and AI may help improve cancer screening and diagnosis and plan treatment.
Macrophage Cell		A type of white blood cell that surrounds and kills microorganisms, removes dead cells and stimulates the actions of other immune cells.
Magnetic Nanoparticle Hyperthermia		Targeted therapeutic heating of tumours in which body tissue is exposed to temperatures above body temperature, in the region of 40-45 °C.
Magnetic Resonance Imaging	MRI	A type of scan that uses strong magnetic fields and radio waves to produce detailed images of the inside of the body.
Magnetic Resonance Perfusion Imaging	MRPI	A special type of magnetic resonance imaging that uses an injected dye in order to see blood flow through tissues. Also called perfusion magnetic resonance imaging.
Magnetic Resonance Spectroscopic Imaging	MRSI	A non-invasive imaging method that provides information about cellular activity (metabolic information). It is used along with MRI to provide information about the shape and size of the tumour (spatial information). Also called proton magnetic resonance spectroscopic imaging.

Term		Definition
Maintenance Therapy		Treatment that is given to help keep cancer from coming back after it has disappeared following the initial therapy. It may include treatment with drugs, vaccines, or antibodies that kill cancer cells, and it may be given for a long time.
Malignancy		See Cancer.
Malignant Tumour		A tumour that has the ability to spread to other parts of the body.
Margin		The edge or border of the tissue removed in cancer surgery. The margin is described as: • negative or clean when the pathologist finds no cancer cells at the edge of the tissue, suggesting that all of the cancer has been removed, or • positive or involved when the pathologist finds cancer cells at the edge of the tissue, suggesting that all of the cancer has not been removed.
Marketing Authorisation		A medicinal product may only be placed on the market in the EEA when a marketing authorisation has been issued by the competent authority of a Member State (or EEA country) for its own territory (national authorisation) or when an authorisation has been granted in accordance with Regulation (EC) No 726/2004 for the entire Community (a Community authorisation).
Marketing Authorisation Holder		The entity that has been granted a Marketing Authorisation. Marketing Authorisation Holders must be established within the EEA.
Masking		See Blinding.
Mass		See Tumour.

Term		Definition
Massively Parallel Sequencing	MPS	A method used in the lab to learn the order of building blocks (called nucleotides) for millions of DNA or RNA fragments at the same time. Computers are used to piece together the fragments in order to sequence a person or other organism's entire DNA, large segments of DNA or RNA, or the DNA in specific types of cells from a sample of tissue. Also called next-generation sequencing.
Maximum Tolerated Dose	MTD	The highest dose of a drug or treatment that does not cause unacceptable side effects. The MTD is determined in clinical trials by testing increasing doses on different groups of people until the highest dose with acceptable side effects is found.
Measurable Disease		A tumour that can be accurately measured in size. This information can be used to judge response to treatment.
Measurable Residual Disease		See Minimal Residual Disease.
Mechanism of Action	MOA	In medicine, a term used to describe how a drug or other substance produces an effect in the body. For example, a drug's mechanism of action could be how it affects a specific target in a cell, such as an enzyme, or a cell function, such as cell growth. Knowing the mechanism of action of a drug may help provide information about the safety of the drug and how it affects the body. It may also help identify the right dose of a drug and which patients are most likely to respond to treatment.

Term	Definition
Median Overall Survival	The length of time from either the date of diagnosis or the start of treatment for a disease, such as cancer, that half of the patients in a group of patients diagnosed with the disease are still alive. In a clinical trial, measuring the median overall survival is one way to see how well a new treatment works. Also called median survival.
Medical Device	Any instrument, apparatus, implement, machine, appliance, implant, software, material, or other similar or related article a) intended by the manufacturer to be used, alone or in combination, for human beings for one or more of the specific purpose(s) of • diagnosis, prevention, monitoring, treatment or alleviation of disease, • diagnosis, monitoring, treatment, alleviation of, or compensation for, an injury, • investigation, replacement, modification, or support of the anatomy or of a physiological process, • supporting or sustaining life, • control of conception, • disinfection of medical devices, and b) which does not achieve its primary intended action in or on the human body by pharmacological, immunological or metabolic means, but which may be assisted in its intended function by such means.

Term		Definition
Medical History		A record of information about a person's health.
		A personal medical history may include information about allergies, illnesses, surgeries, immunisations, and results of physical exams and tests.
		It may also include information about medicines taken and health habits, such as diet and exercise.
		A family medical history includes health information about a person's close family members (parents, grandparents, children, brothers, and sisters).
		This includes their current and past illnesses.
		A family medical history may show a pattern of certain diseases in a family.
		Also called health history.
Medical Nutrition Therapy		Treatment based on nutrition.
		It includes checking a person's nutrition status and giving the right foods or nutrients to treat conditions such as those caused by diabetes, heart disease, and cancer.
		It may involve simple changes in a person's diet, or intravenous or tube feeding.
		Medical nutrition therapy may help patients recover more quickly and spend less time in the hospital.
		Also called nutrition therapy.
Medical Oncologist		A doctor who has special training in diagnosing and treating cancer in adults using chemotherapy, hormonal therapy, biological therapy, and targeted therapy.
		A medical oncologist often is the main healthcare provider for someone who has cancer.
		A medical oncologist also gives supportive care and may coordinate treatment given by other specialists.

Term		Definition
Medical Research Council	MRC	The body responsible for coordinating and funding medical research in the United Kingdom.
Medication		A dosage form that contains one or more active and/or inactive ingredients. Medications come in many dosage forms, including tablets, capsules, liquids, creams, and patches. They can also be given in different ways, such as by mouth, by infusion into a vein, or by drops that are put into the ear or eye. The form with the active ingredient is used to prevent, diagnose, treat, or relieve symptoms of a disease or abnormal condition. A medication that does not contain an active ingredient and is used in research studies is called a placebo (see Placebo).
Medicine		The practices and procedures used for the prevention, treatment, or relief of symptoms of diseases or abnormal conditions. This term may also refer to a legal drug used for the same purpose.
Medicines and Healthcare Products Regulatory Agency	MHRA	The government agency responsible for ensuring that medicines and medical devices work and are safe.
Medicines for Human Use	MHU	The Medicines for Human Use (Clinical Trials) Regulation is the UK response to the European Union Clinical Trials Directive 2001/20EC. It covers the legal requirements for clinical trials involving an investigational medicinal product.
Mega-voltage Linear Accelerator		See Linac.

Term		Definition
Meiosis		A type of cell division in sexually reproducing organisms that reduces the number of chromosomes in gametes (the sex cells, or egg and sperm).
Mental Capacity Act (2005)		A statutory framework to empower and protect vulnerable people who are not able to make their own decisions. It makes it clear who can make decisions, in which situations, and how they should go about this. The research provisions of the Mental Capacity Act 2005 do not apply to the conduct of CTIMPs.
Messenger RNA	mRNA	A type of RNA found in cells. mRNA molecules carry the genetic information needed to make proteins. They carry the information from the DNA in the nucleus of the cell to the cytoplasm where the proteins are made.
Meta-Analysis		A comparison using multiple independent pieces of prior research, such as clinical trials, that investigated the same research question. Results are combined across the sources of research to provide an overall conclusion to the research question of interest.
Metadata		Summarises basic information about data (for example, author, date created, date modified and file size).
Metal Prosthesis		An artificial metal device that replaces a missing body part, which may be lost through physical trauma, disease, or a condition present at birth (congenital disorder). Prostheses are intended to restore the normal functions of the missing body part.

Term		Definition
Metastasis		The spread of cancer from the place where it began (primary tumour) to another part of the body. Cancer cells can break away and travel around the body through the blood or lymphatic system. The cells form new tumours where they settle and grow.
Metastasis-free Survival	MFS	The length of time from the start of treatment for cancer that a patient is still alive and the cancer has not spread to other parts of the body. In a clinical trial, measuring the metastasis-free survival is one way to see how well a new treatment works.
Methodology		Describes decisions made about what data will be collected, from whom, and how it will be collected and analysed. It also describes why a particular method has been chosen.
Metronomic Chemotherapy		See Low-dose Chemotherapy.
MeV Linear Accelerator		See Linac.
Microarray		A laboratory tool used to analyse large numbers of genes or proteins at one time. In a microarray, biological molecules such as DNA, RNA, or protein are placed in a pattern onto a surface such as a glass slide. Other substances can be added to these slides to detect specific patterns of molecules. Microarrays are being used to help diagnose diseases, such as cancer, and to develop treatments for them.
Micro-metastasis		Small numbers of cancer cells that have spread from the primary tumour to other parts of the body and are too few to be picked up in a screening or diagnostic test.

Term		Definition
Micro Ribonucleic Acid	miRNA	A type of RNA found in cells and in blood. miRNA are smaller than many other types of RNA and can bind to messenger RNAs (mRNAs) to block them from making proteins. miRNA is being studied in the diagnosis and treatment of cancer.
Microsatellite		A short sequence of DNA, usually 1 to 4 base pairs (a unit of DNA), that is repeated together in a row along the DNA molecule. There is variation from person to person in the number of repeats. There are hundreds of places in human DNA that contain microsatellites.
Microsatellite Instability (-high)	MSI (-H)	Describes cancer cells that have a high number of mutations (changes) within microsatellites. Microsatellite testing that shows mutations in 30% or more microsatellites is called microsatellite instability-high. MIS-h cancer cells may have a defect in the ability to correct mistakes that occur when DNA is copied in the cell. Knowing whether cancer is microsatellite instability-high may help plan the best treatment.
Microsatellite Tumours		A small group of tumour cells in an area beside or below, but separate from, the primary (original) melanoma. Microsatellite tumours can only be seen with a microscope. Having a microsatellite tumour is a sign that the melanoma has spread from where it first formed.
Microscopic Anatomy		See Histology.

Term		Definition
Microwave Ablation	MWA	Microwave ablation is a form of thermal ablation used in interventional radiology to treat cancer. MWA uses electromagnetic waves in the microwave energy spectrum to produce tissue-heating effects.
Microwave Thermotherapy		See Microwave Therapy.
Microwave Therapy		A type of treatment in which body tissue is exposed to high temperatures to damage and kill cancer cells or to make cancer cells more sensitive to the effects of radiation and certain anti-cancer drugs. Also called microwave thermotherapy.
Minimally Invasive Surgery		Surgery that is carried out using small incisions (cuts) and few stitches. During minimally invasive surgery, one or more small incisions may be made in the body. A laparoscope (thin, tube-like instrument with a light and a lens for viewing) is inserted through one opening to guide the surgery. Tiny surgical instruments are inserted through other openings to carry out the surgery. Minimally invasive surgery may cause less pain, scarring, and damage to healthy tissue, and the patient may have a faster recovery than with traditional surgery.

Term		Definition
Minimal Residual Disease		A term used to describe a very small number of cancer cells that remain in the body during or after treatment. Minimal residual disease can be found only by highly sensitive laboratory methods that are able to find one cancer cell among one million normal cells. Checking to see if there is minimal residual disease may help plan treatment, find out how well treatment is working or if cancer has come back, or make a prognosis. Also called measurable residual disease.
Minor		In relation to a CTIMP, defined in 'The Medicines for Human Use (Clinical Trials) Regulations' as a person under the age of 16.
Mismatch Repair (Deficiency)	MMR	Describes cells that have mutations (changes) in certain genes that are involved in correcting mistakes made when DNA is copied in a cell. MMR-deficient cells usually have many DNA mutations, which may lead to cancer. Knowing if a tumour is MMR-deficient may help plan treatment or predict how well the tumour will respond to treatment. Also called deficient DNA mismatch repair and deficient mismatch repair.
Mitochondria		Small structures in a cell that are found in the cytoplasm (the fluid that surrounds the cell nucleus). Mitochondria make most of the energy for the cell and have their own genetic material that is different to the genetic material found in the nucleus. Many diseases are caused by mutations (changes) in the DNA of mitochondria.

Term		Definition
Mitosis		The process by which a cell replicates its chromosomes and then segregates them, producing two identical nuclei in preparation for cell division. Mitosis is generally followed by an equal division of the cell's content into two daughter cells that have identical genomes.
Mitotic Rate	MR	A measure of how fast cancer cells are dividing and growing. To find the MR, the number of cells dividing in a certain amount of cancer tissue is counted. MR is used to help find the stage of melanoma (a type of skin cancer) and other types of cancer. Higher MRs are linked with lower survival rates.
Modality		A method of treatment. For example, surgery and chemotherapy are treatment modalities.
Molecular Characterisation		A broad term that refers to using molecular markers, including DNA, RNA, and proteins, to determine the genetic characteristics of cells or tissues. In cancer, molecular characterisation may provide information about the presence of certain biomarkers or genetic changes in tumour tissue, such as gene mutations, patterns of gene expression, and other changes in tumour DNA or RNA. Molecular characterisation can play an important role in how diseases, such as cancer, are diagnosed and treated and how they respond to treatment. Genomic sequencing, molecular profiling, and liquid biopsy are all types of molecular characterisation.

Term		Definition
Molecular Diagnostics		Laboratory methods that are used to help identify a disease or the risk of developing a disease, such as cancer, by studying molecules, such as DNA, RNA, and proteins, in a tissue or fluid sample. Molecular diagnostics may also be used to help plan treatment for a disease, look for recurrence of disease, or find out how well treatment is working. There are many types of molecular diagnostic tests, such as biomarker tests, genetic tests, tumour sequencing tests, and liquid biopsies.
Molecular Gene		A sequence of nucleotides in DNA that is transcribed to produce a functional RNA. There are two types of molecular genes: • protein-coding genes, and • non-coding genes.
Molecular Marker		See Biomarker
Molecular Medicine		A branch of medicine that develops ways to diagnose and treat disease by understanding the way genes, proteins, and other cellular molecules work. Molecular medicine is based on research that shows how certain genes, molecules, and cellular functions may become abnormal in diseases such as cancer.
Molecular Radiation Therapy		A type of radiation therapy in which a radionuclide (a radioactive chemical) is linked to a cell-targeting molecule, such as a monoclonal antibody, and injected into the body. The cell-targeting molecule binds to a specific target found on some cancer cells. This may help kill the targeted cancer cells whilst limiting the harm to normal cells. Also called targeted radionuclide therapy.

Term		Definition
Molecular Risk Assessment		A procedure in which biomarkers. For example, biological molecules or changes in tumour cell DNA are used to estimate a person's risk of developing cancer. Specific biomarkers may be linked to particular types of cancer.
Molecular Subtype		In cancer, a term used to describe the smaller groups that a type of cancer can be divided into, based on whether certain genetic changes or other biomarkers are present. For example, breast cancer can be broken down into several molecular subtypes based on whether the cancer cells have oestrogen receptors (ER), progesterone receptors (PR), or HER2 on their surface. Knowing the molecular subtype of a cancer may help plan treatment, find out how well treatment is working, or make a prognosis.
Molecular target		In cancer, a term used to describe certain genes, proteins, and other molecules that are involved in the growth, spread, and survival of cancer cells and may be used as targets for cancer treatment. Treatments that block molecular targets or the signals they send may kill cancer cells or keep cancer cells from growing or spreading.

Term		Definition
Molecularly Targeted Therapies	MTT	A type of treatment that uses drugs or other substances to target specific molecules that cancer cells need to survive and spread. Molecularly targeted therapies work in different ways to treat cancer. Some stop cancer cells from growing by interrupting signals that cause them to grow and divide, stopping signals that help form blood vessels, delivering cell-killing substances to cancer cells, or starving cancer cells of hormones they need to grow. Other molecularly targeted therapies help the immune system kill cancer cells or directly cause cancer cell death. Most molecularly targeted therapies are either small-molecule drugs or monoclonal antibodies. Also called targeted therapy.
Monitor		See Clinical Research Associate.
Monitoring		The act of overseeing the progress of a clinical trial, and of ensuring that it is conducted and recorded in accordance with the protocol, Standard Operating Procedures (SOPs), Good Clinical Practice (GCP) and the applicable regulatory requirement(s).
Monitoring Report		A written report from the monitor to the sponsor after each site visit and/or other trial-related communication according to the sponsor's SOPs.

Term		Definition
Monocyte		A type of immune cell that is made in the bone marrow and travels through the blood to tissues in the body where it becomes a macrophage or a dendritic cell. Macrophages surround and kill microorganisms, ingest foreign material, remove dead cells, and boost immune responses. During inflammation, dendritic cells boost immune responses by showing antigens on their surface to other cells of the immune system. A monocyte is a type of white blood cell and a type of phagocyte.
Monotherapy		Therapy that uses one type of treatment, such as radiation therapy or surgery alone, to treat a certain disease or condition. In drug therapy, monotherapy refers to the use of a single drug to treat a disease or condition.
Morbidity		The state of having an illness, disease or medical condition.
Mortality (Rate)		The number of deaths in a particular population during a certain time.
MRI Ultrasound Fusion-guided Biopsy		See Fusion biopsy.
Multi-cancer Detection (test)	MCD	A type of blood test that is being studied as a way to screen for many types of cancer at the same time. Also known as multi-cancer early detection tests.
Multi-cancer Early Detection (test)	MCED	See Multi-cancer Detection test.
Multicentre Trial		A trial which takes place at more than one site (usually a hospital). Also known as a multi-site trial.

Term		Definition
Multidisciplinary team	MDT	A group of professionals from one or more clinical disciplines who together make decisions regarding the treatment of individual patients.
Multifactorial Disease		See Complex Disease.
Multi-gated Acquisition (scan)	MUGA	A MUGA scan is an imaging test to see how your heart pumps blood. It measures a percentage called ejection fraction (EF). Your EF is the percentage of blood that your heart pumps out each time it contracts.
Multigene Panel Test	MGPT	A laboratory test in which many genes are studied in a sample of tissue. MGPTs help find mutations (changes) in certain genes that may increase a person's risk of a disease such as cancer. They may also look at the activity of certain genes in a sample of tissue. MGPTs may be used to help plan treatment or help predict whether cancer will spread to other parts of the body or come back. Also called the multigene test.
Multigene Test		See Multigene Panel Test.
Multimodality Therapy		Therapy that combines more than one method of treatment. Also called combination therapy and multimodality treatment.
Multimodality Treatment		See Multimodality Therapy.
Multiple Primary Cancers		See Multiple Primary Malignancies.
Multiple Primary Malignancies	MPM	Multiple primary malignancies refer to two or more different primary cancers in the same patient occurring in the same or different organs or tissues. Also known as multiple primary cancers.
Multi-site Trial		See Multicentre Trial.

Term		Definition
Mutagen		Anything that causes a mutation (a change in the DNA of a cell). DNA changes caused by mutagens may harm cells and cause certain diseases, such as cancer. Examples of mutagens include radioactive substances, X-rays, ultraviolet radiation, and certain chemicals.
Mutation		Cancers are caused by a change in, or damage to, one or more genes. Most changes in a gene are because of a gene mutation. Mutations can stop genes from working properly. Genes that have mutations that are linked to cancer are sometimes called cancer genes. Also called a variant.

N

Term		Definition
Nanoparticle		Nanoparticles are spherical, polymeric particles composed of natural or artificial polymers. Nanoparticles are being studied in the detection, diagnosis and treatment of cancer.
Nanopore DNA Sequencing		A laboratory technique for determining the exact sequence of nucleotides, or bases, in a DNA molecule.
Nanoprobe		A device that uses X-rays instead of visible light to form images of very small structures, such as the insides of blood vessels and cells. It can be used to study processes such as angiogenesis (growth of blood vessels). The term nanoprobe is also used to describe very small particles that can be used in the detection, diagnosis, and treatment of cancer.
Nanotechnology		The field of research that deals with the engineering and creation of things from materials that are less than 100 nanometres (one-billionth of a meter) in size, especially single atoms or molecules. Nanotechnology is being studied in the detection, diagnosis, and treatment of cancer.
National Cancer Institute	NCI	The National Cancer Institute, part of the National Institutes of Health of the United States Department of Health and Human Services, is the US Federal Government's principal agency for cancer research. The NCI conducts, coordinates, and funds cancer research, training, health information dissemination, and other programs with respect to the cause, diagnosis, prevention, and treatment of cancer.
National Cancer Institute-Common Terminology Criteria for Adverse Events	NCI-CTCAE	A descriptive terminology which can be used for Adverse Event (AE) reporting. A severity scale is provided for each AE term.

Term		Definition
National Cancer Registration and Analysis Service	NCRAS	NCRAS provides near-real-time, cost-effective, comprehensive, quality-assured data services covering the entire cancer pathway of all patients in England.
National Health Service	NHS	The UK Government-funded medical and health care services which are free to those living in the UK.
National Health Service Permission		NHS Permission for research (formerly known as R&D Approval) confirms that appropriate checks have been made and that clinical negligence will be covered by NHS indemnity schemes or by independent contractors' professional indemnity insurance during the course of the research. In addition, where the staff of an NHS organisation were responsible for designing the study, NHS permission confirms that indemnity is provided for harm arising from the design of the study. NHS permission for research ensures that: • The organisation is aware of the potential impact of the research in terms of risks and resources. • The organisation has made the necessary arrangements to support the activity. • All the activities for which the organisation is responsible are compliant with the law. • The organisation accepts vicarious liability for the activities of staff for which it is responsible.
National Health Service Permission		Letter confirming that NHS Permission has been given and the study can commence. Similar terms are used for the permission letter issued in other UK countries.
National Health Service R&D Office		The responsible person or team acting on behalf of the NHS in matters relating to R&D management. The NHS R&D Office may delegate some of its functions to other parties. NB. Where a trial is run without NHS involvement, the term NHS R&D office may often be replaced with the term 'sponsor's office'.

226

Term		Definition
National Institute for Health Research	NIHR	The health research system funded by the Department of Health to improve the health of the population through research. The NIHR provides substantial funding for many clinical trials to support important medical research.
National Institute for Health Research Biomedical Research Centre	NIHR BRC	NIHR BRCs are collaborations between world-leading universities and NHS organisations that bring together academics and clinicians to translate lab-based scientific breakthroughs into potential new treatments, diagnostics and medical technologies.
National Institute for Health Research Clinical Research Facility	NIHR CRF	NIHR CRFs (for Experimental Medicine) are dedicated facilities where specialist clinical research and support staff from universities and NHS Trusts work together on patient-orientated commercial and non-commercial experimental medicine studies. CRFs are designed to support high-intensity studies and overnight stays.
National Institute for Health Research Clinical Research Network	NIHR CRN	The NIHR CRN is made up of 15 Local Clinical Research Networks that cover the length and breadth of England. These local networks coordinate and support the delivery of research in the NHS and across the wider health and social care environment in England.
National Institute for Health Research Experimental Cancer Medicine Centre	NIHR ECMC	The NIHR ECMCs act as an efficient and effective UK-wide network for delivering pioneering, early-phase cancer trials, bringing together world-leading laboratory and clinical researchers to test new treatments for adults and children with cancer.
National Institute for Health Research Invention for Innovation	NIHR i4i	The NIHR Invention for Innovation Programme is a translational research funding scheme aimed at medical devices, in vitro diagnostic devices and digital health technologies addressing an existing or emerging health or social care need.

Term		Definition
National Institute for Health Research Support Service	NIHR RSS	The NIHR RSS provides free and confidential advice to develop funding applications within the remit of the NIHR, including clinical, applied health and social care research, and post-award advice to award holders.
National Research Ethics Service	NRES	The NRES is a part of the Health Research Authority (HRA). The NRES has two roles: • to protect the rights, safety, dignity and well-being of research participants, and • to facilitate and promote ethical research that is of potential benefit to participants, science and society.
Natural Killer Cell		A type of immune cell that has granules (small particles) with enzymes that can kill tumour cells or cells infected with a virus. A natural killer cell is a type of white blood cell.
Negative Predictive Value	NPV	The likelihood that a person who has a negative test result indeed does not have the disease, condition, biomarker, or mutation (change) in the gene being tested. The negative predictive value is a way of measuring how accurate a specific test is.
Neoadjuvant Therapy		Treatment given before the main treatment. For example, chemotherapy before surgery may shrink the tumour so that it is easier to remove.
Neoplasm		See Tumour.
Neuron		Neurons are electrically excitable cells that transmit signals throughout the body. Neurons employ both electrical and chemical components in the transmission of information. Neurons are connected to other neurons at synapses and connected to effector organs or cells at neuroeffector junctions.

Term		Definition
Neutrophil		Neutrophils are a type of white blood cell. They form the most abundant type of granulocytes and makeup 40% to 70% of all white blood cells in humans. They form an essential part of the innate immune system
New Mutation		See De novo Mutation.
New Variant		See De novo Mutation.
Next-generation Sequencing		See Massively Parallel Sequencing.
Nocebo Effect		A situation in which a patient develops side effects or symptoms that can occur with a drug or other therapy just because the patient believes they may occur. For example, in a clinical trial, patients who are not given an active treatment, but are told what side effects the active treatment may cause, may have the same side effects as the patients who are given the active treatment, only because they expect them to occur.
Node Negative		Cancer that has not spread to the lymph nodes.
Node Positive		Cancer that has spread to the lymph nodes.
Nodule		See Tumour.
Nomogram		A mathematical device or model that shows relationships between things. For example, a nomogram of height and weight measurements can be used to find the surface area of a person, without doing the math, to determine the right dose of chemotherapy. Nomograms of patient and disease characteristics can help predict the outcome of some kinds of cancer.
Nonblinded		Describes a clinical trial or other experiment in which the researchers know what treatments are being given to each study subject or experimental group. If human subjects are involved, they know what treatments they are receiving.

Term		Definition
Non-Clinical Trial of an Investigational Medicinal Product	Non-CTIMP	Trials that do not involve an Investigational Medicinal Product (IMP) as defined by the MHRA, and therefore do not fall within the scope of the Medicines for Human Use (Clinical Trials) Regulations 2004.
Nonheritable		In medicine, describes a characteristic or trait that cannot be passed from a parent to a child through the genes. Nonheritable forms of cancer may occur when there is a mutation (change) in the DNA in any of the cells of the body, except the germ cells (sperm and egg). People who have a nonheritable form of cancer do not have a family history of that cancer or an inherited change in their DNA that would increase their risk for that cancer.
Non-Inferiority Trial		A trial designed to show that the effect of a new treatment is not worse than the standard treatment. Non-inferiority trials are sometimes carried out when a placebo (an inactive treatment) cannot be used. These trials may show that a new treatment (such as a drug) is not worse than the active treatment being compared, and it may be safer and easier to take or cause fewer side effects.

Term		Definition
Non-Interventional Trial		A study of one or more medicinal products which have a marketing authorisation, where the following conditions are met: • The products are prescribed in the usual manner in accordance with the terms of that authorisation • The assignment of any patient involved in the study to a particular therapeutic strategy is not decided in advance by a protocol but falls within current practice • The decision to prescribe a particular medicinal product is clearly separated from the decision to include the patient in the study • No diagnostic or monitoring procedures are applied to the patients included in the study, other than those which are ordinarily applied in the course of the particular therapeutic strategy in question, and • Epidemiological methods are to be used for the analysis of the data arising from the study.
Non-invasive		In medicine, it describes a procedure that does not require inserting an instrument through the skin or into a body opening. In cancer, it describes a disease that has not spread outside the tissue in which it began.
Non-Investigational Medicinal Product	NIMP	A medicinal product which is not classed as an IMP in a trial but may be taken by subjects during the trial. Examples include concomitant or rescue/escape medication used for preventive, diagnostic or therapeutic reasons and/or medication given to ensure that adequate medical care is provided for the subject during a trial.
Non-malignant		Not cancer. Non-malignant tumours may grow larger but do not spread to other parts of the body. Also called benign.

Term	Definition
Nonpenetrant	A term that describes when a person has a disease-causing mutation (change) in a gene but never develops the disease. For example, a woman may have a certain BRCA1 gene mutation that increases her risk of breast cancer, but because the gene mutation is nonpenetrant, she never develops breast cancer. However, she can still pass the BRCA1 gene mutation to her children, who may develop cancer.
Nonsense Mutation	A sequence change that gives rise to a stop codon rather than a codon specifying an amino acid.
Normal Range	In medicine, a set of values that a doctor uses to interpret a patient's test results. The normal range for a given test is based on the results that are seen in 95% of the healthy population. Sometimes patients whose test results are outside of the normal range may be healthy, and some patients whose test results are within the normal range may have a health problem. The normal range for a test may be different for different groups of people (for example, men and women). Also called reference interval, reference range, and reference values.
Nuclear Grade	An evaluation of the size and shape of the nucleus in tumour cells and the percentage of tumour cells that are in the process of dividing or growing. Cancers with low nuclear grade grow and spread less quickly than cancers with high nuclear grade.
Nuclear Medicine	The branch of medicine that deals with the use of radioactive substances in research, diagnosis, and treatment.
Nucleotide	A compound consisting of a nucleoside linked to a phosphate group. Nucleotides form the basic structural unit of nucleic acids such as DNA.
Nutrition Therapy	See Medical Nutrition Therapy.

O

Term		Definition
Objective Improvement		An improvement that can be measured. For example, when a tumour shrinks or there are fewer cancer cells in the blood.
Objective Response Rate	ORR	The percentage of people in a study or treatment group who have a partial response or complete response to the treatment within a certain period of time. A partial response is a decrease in the size of a tumour or in the amount of cancer in the body, and a complete response is the disappearance of all signs of cancer in the body. In a clinical trial, measuring the ORR is one way to see how well a new treatment works.
Observational Study		A study which investigates health outcomes amongst groups of people in the course of their everyday life. In these studies, researchers do not intervene; they collect data through observation only.
Occult Primary Tumour		Cancer in which the site of the primary (original) tumour cannot be found. Most metastases from occult primary tumours are found in the head and neck.
Octreotide Scan		See Somatostatin Receptor Scintigraphy.

Term	Definition
Odds Ratio	A measure of the odds of an event happening in one group compared to the odds of the same event happening in another group.
	In cancer research, odds ratios are most often used in case-control (backward-looking) studies to find out if being exposed to a certain substance or other factor increases the risk of cancer. For example, researchers may study a group of individuals with cancer (cases) and another group without cancer (controls) to see how many people in each group were exposed to a certain substance or factor.
	They calculate the odds of exposure in both groups and then compare the odds.
	Also called relative odds.
Off-Target Effect	Describes the effects that can occur when a drug binds to targets (proteins or other molecules in the body) other than those for which the drug was meant to bind.
	This can lead to unexpected side effects that may be harmful.
	Learning about the off-target effects of drugs may help in drug development.
Oligometastatic Cancer	An intermediate stage of cancer between localised and widely spread disease, a subclass of stage IV cancer.
	If you have oligometastatic cancer, that means cancer has spread to fewer than five sites in the body.

Term		Definition
Oncogene		A mutated (changed) form of a type of gene called a proto-oncogene, which is involved in normal cell growth and division. When a proto-oncogene is changed so that too many copies are made or it becomes more active than normal, it is called an oncogene. Mutations that lead to the conversion of proto-oncogenes to oncogenes usually occur during a person's lifetime and are not inherited from a parent. Oncogenes may cause normal cells to become cancer cells and grow in the body.
Oncologist		A specialist doctor who provides medical care for a person diagnosed with cancer.
Oncology		The study of cancer.
Oncolysis		The lysis (breakdown) of cancer cells. This can be caused by chemical or physical means (for example, strong detergents or high-energy sound waves) or by infection with a strain of virus that can lyse cells.
Open-Label Study		A trial where both the investigators and the patients know which treatment is to be given.
Organ		A human organ is a collection of tissues that structurally form a functional unit specialised to perform a particular function in the human body. The heart, kidneys, and lungs are examples of organs.
Organ System		An organ system is a biological system consisting of a group of organs that work together to perform one or more functions.
Outcome Measure		A pre-determined measurement designed to assess the effect of a clinical trial intervention.

Term		Definition
Overall Survival	OS	The length of time from either the date of diagnosis or the start of treatment for a disease, such as cancer, that patients diagnosed with the disease are still alive. In a clinical trial, measuring the overall survival is one way to see how well a new treatment works.
Overall Survival Rate		See Survival Rate.
Overdiagnosis		Finding cases of cancer with a screening test (such as a mammogram or PSA test) that will never cause any symptoms. These cancers may just stop growing or go away on their own. Some of the harms caused by overdiagnosis are anxiety and having treatment that is not needed.
Overtreatment		Unnecessary treatment for a condition that is not life-threatening or would never cause any symptoms. Overtreatment may lead to problems and harmful side effects. Overtreatment can be a result of overdiagnosis.

P

Term		Definition
Palliative Care		Treatment given to patients with incurable disease to reduce that patient's symptoms or treatment side effects. Also called supportive care.
Palpable Disease		A term used to describe cancer that can be felt by touch, usually present in lymph nodes, skin, or other organs of the body such as the liver or colon.
Parallel Design		A clinical trial design where two or more groups of participants receive different interventions. For example, a two-arm parallel design involves two groups of participants. One group receives drug A, and the other group receives drug B, and the results are compared.
Participant		An individual who consents to take part in a trial. In law, participants in clinical trials involving medicinal products or control are referenced as subjects. Also known as a Subject.
Participant Identification Centre	PIC	Organisations which refer potential participants to a research team at another organisation, but do not conduct trial-related activity themselves. If activities such as consent take place, then the site would not be classed as a PIC.
Participant Information Sheet	PIS	A document for potential trial participants to help them understand the expectations and requirements of participation in a clinical trial.
Passive Immunity		Passive immunity occurs when a person receives antibodies to a disease or toxin rather than making them through their own immune system.
Pathogen		Any organism or agent that can produce disease. A pathogen may also be referred to as an infectious agent, or simply a germ.
Pathogenic Variant		See Predisposing Mutation.

Term		Definition
Pathologic Complete Remission		The lack of all signs of cancer in tissue samples removed during surgery or biopsy after treatment with radiation or chemotherapy.
		To find out if there is a pathologic complete remission, a pathologist checks the tissue samples under a microscope to see if there are still cancer cells left after the anti-cancer treatment.
		Knowing if the cancer is in pathologic complete remission may help show how well treatment is working or if the cancer will come back.
		Also called pathologic complete response.
Pathologic Complete Response		See Pathologic Complete Remission.
Pathologist		A doctor who specialises in interpreting laboratory tests to diagnose disease.
Pathology Report		A pathology report provides the definitive cancer diagnosis.
		It is also used for staging (describing the extent of cancer within the body, especially whether it has spread) and to help plan treatment.
Patient Advocate		An advocate who uses their lived experience (of cancer) to help shape research.
Patient and Public Involvement	PPI	PPI is where research is designed and carried out with the input of:
		• People with lived experience of the condition being investigated (patients), or
		• Members of the public.
Patient and Public Involvement and Engagement	PPIE	In addition to PPI activities advocates assist researchers in raising awareness of research and research trial results with members of the public.
Patient Information Sheet	PIS	A detailed guide to a research trial, written in lay terms, with information regarding participation in the trial.
		Also called a Patient Information Leaflet (PIL).
Patient Reported Outcome (Measures)	PRO(M)	Patients' perspectives about the impact of disease and treatment on their own health.

Term		Definition
Peer Review		The review of a clinical trial by experts chosen by the Study Sponsor. These experts review the trials for scientific merit, participants' safety and ethical considerations.
Penetrance		Describes how likely it is that a person who has a certain disease-causing mutation (change) in a gene will show signs and symptoms of the disease. Not everyone who has the mutation will develop the disease. For example, some people who have a BRCA1 or BRCA2 gene mutation will develop cancer during their lifetime, but others will not. Complete penetrance means that every person who has the mutation will show signs and symptoms of the disease. Currently, there is no way of knowing which people who have a cancer-causing mutation will develop cancer.
Peptide		A short chain of amino acids (typically 2 to 50) linked by chemical bonds (called peptide bonds).
Perfusion Magnetic Resonance Imaging	PMRI	See Magnetic Resonance Perfusion Imaging.
Pharmacodynamics		The study of a drug's molecular, biochemical, and physiologic effects or actions.
Pharmacogenomics		A component of genomic medicine that involves using a patient's genomic information to tailor the selection of drugs used in their medical management. In this way, pharmacogenomics aims to provide a more individualised (or precise) approach to the use of available medication in treating patients.
Pharmacokinetics	PK	Pharmacokinetics is a branch of pharmacology dedicated to describing how the body affects a specific substance after administration.
Pharmacologic		Relating to pharmacology
Pharmacology		The scientific study of the effects of drugs and chemicals on living organisms.

Term		Definition
Pharma-covigilance	PV	The science relating to the detection, assessment, understanding and prevention of the adverse effects of medicines.
Phase		Clinical trials follow certain steps called 'phases'. There are four phases of clinical trials, and each is designed to ask specific questions about the intervention or drug being tested. The intervention or drug must be successfully tested in 3 phases (phases 1-3) to be approved for use in the general population.
Phase 0 (also known as Early Phase 1)		Exploratory trials sometimes run before traditional phase 1 trials to check that a low dose of treatment is not harmful. Usually 10-20 people.
Phase 1 (I) Trial		Phase 1 trials investigate whether a treatment is safe for people to take, to find the best dose, and to find out if there are any side effects. In cancer trials, phase 1 participants are cancer patients. Usually 20-50 people. Categorised as Human Pharmacology.
Phase 2 (II) Trial		Phase 2 trials aim to check the best dose and learn more about side effects, whilst looking at the effectiveness of treatment too. Usually 100-300 people. Categorised as Therapeutic Exploratory.
Phase 3 (III) Trial		If previous trials have indicated a treatment is safe and effective, phase 3 trials will begin. Phase 3 trials test the new intervention against standard treatments, or a 'dummy drug' (placebo). Usually, several hundred to several thousand patients. Categorised as Therapeutic Confirmatory.
Phase 4 (IV) Trial		A phase of research to describe clinical trials occurring after a drug has been approved for marketing. These trials gather additional information about a drug's long-term safety, efficacy or optimal use. Categorised as Therapeutic Use.

Term		Definition
Photodynamic Therapy		A form of phototherapy involving light and a photosensitising chemical substance used in conjunction with molecular oxygen to elicit cell death.
Photon Beam Radiotherapy		A type of radiation therapy that uses x-rays or gamma rays that come from a special machine called a linear accelerator (Linac). The radiation dose is delivered at the surface of the body and goes into the tumour and through the body. Photon beam radiation therapy is different to proton beam therapy.
Pilot Study		A pilot study is a smaller version of the main study used to test whether the main study can work on a larger scale. For example, to ensure that recruitment, randomisation, treatment, and follow-up assessments all run smoothly.
Placebo		A placebo is an inactive control substance (a dummy treatment) that allows researchers to test for the 'placebo effect'. It is a psychological response where patients feel better even though the substance that they are taking has no effect. By comparing people's responses to the placebo and to the drug being tested, researchers can tell whether the drug is having any real benefit. In cancer clinical trials placebos are rarely used, although they may be used when there is no standard treatment available.
Plain English Summary		A clear, brief summary of the research that has been written for members of the public, rather than researchers or professionals.

Term		Definition
Plasma		Plasma is the part of the blood that carries platelets, red blood cells and white blood cells around the body. It contains antibodies, known as immunoglobulins, which fight infection. Antibodies are made into life-saving medicines to save and transform lives. Plasma makes up approximately 55% of blood.
Plasma Cell		A type of immune cell that makes large amounts of a specific antibody. Plasma cells develop from B-cells that have been activated. A plasma cell is a type of white blood cell. Also called plasmacyte.
Plasmacyte		See Plasma Cell.
Platelet		Platelets (also known as thrombocytes) are small, colourless cell fragments in the blood that form clots and stop or prevent bleeding. Platelets are made in bone marrow, the sponge-like tissue inside bones.
Platform Trial		A platform trial is a clinical trial with a single master protocol in which multiple treatments are evaluated at the same time. It also allows new treatments to be added and removed from the study without having to pause enrolment or resubmit the entire clinical trial protocol for regulatory review.
Poly Adenosine Diphosphate-ribose Polymerase	PARP	Poly (ADP-ribose) polymerase is a family of proteins involved in a number of cellular processes such as DNA repair, genomic stability, and programmed cell death.
Poly Adenosine Diphosphate-ribose Polymerase Inhibitor	PARP Inhibitor	PARP inhibitors are a group of pharmacological inhibitors of the enzyme poly ADP-ribose polymerase. They are developed for multiple indications, including the treatment of heritable cancers. Several forms of cancer are more dependent on PARP than regular cells, making PARP an attractive target for cancer therapy.

Term		Definition
Polygenic Risk Score	PRS	A PRS uses genomic information in isolation to assess a person's chances of having or developing a particular medical condition. A person's PRS is a statistical calculation based on the presence or absence of multiple genomic variants, without taking environmental or other factors into account.
Polypeptide		A long chain of linked amino acids (51 or more). The proteins manufactured inside cells are made from one or more polypeptides.
Population Research		Population research is the study of causes and patterns of occurrence of cancer and the evaluation of risk. Also known as epidemiological research.
Positron Emission Tomography	PET	A positron emission tomography scan produces detailed 3-D images of the inside of the body.
Post Hoc Analysis		Post hoc analysis consists of looking at the data after the experiment has concluded for patterns that were not specified upfront. Also informally called data dredging.
Post Hoc, Ergo Propter Hoc		Latin *after this, therefore because of this*. The idea that correlation implies causation is an example of a questionable-cause logical fallacy in which one event seems to be the cause of a later event because it occurred earlier and thus has a cause-and-effect relationship. The Bradford Hill criteria are a group of nine principles that can be useful in establishing epidemiologic evidence of a causal relationship. See also cum hoc, ergo propter hoc
Post-Remission Therapy		See Intensification Therapy.

Term		Definition
Power		The probability of detecting a proposed effect if there is one to detect.
		In clinical trials, power is the probability that a trial will detect the proposed effect of the intervention being tested.
		A high power increases confidence that it will show the effect of the intervention (if there is one)—often in comparison to a control treatment (i.e., standard of care).
Pragmatic Trial		A trial that aims to test the effectiveness of a treatment policy in a 'real life' situation.
		This differs from explanatory trials where the effectiveness of an intervention is tested under ideal conditions.
Precancerous (Premalignant)		Refers to cells that are not cancerous but have the potential to become cancerous.
Precision		How close a set of measurements are to each other in value.
Precision Medicine		Precision medicine is medical care designed to optimise efficiency or therapeutic benefit for particular groups of patients, especially by using genetic or molecular profiling.
Predisposing Mutation		A change in the DNA sequence of a gene that causes a person to have or be at risk of developing a certain genetic disorder or disease, such as cancer.
		Predisposing mutations can be inherited from a parent or occur during a person's lifetime.
		Knowing if a person has a predisposing mutation may help prevent, diagnose, and treat diseases, such as cancer.
		Not everyone who has a predisposing mutation will develop the disease.
		Also called deleterious mutation, disease-causing mutation, pathogenic variant, and susceptibility gene mutation.

Term		Definition
Prevalence		Prevalence of cancer is the proportion of people within a population who have cancer at a given time. Prevalence is often described as a percentage. For example, if 5/10 people in a focus group have breast cancer, the prevalence of breast cancer in that focus group is 50%.
Primary Cancer		Describes the location of the original cancer in the case that it has spread elsewhere.
Primary Endpoint		The main result that is measured at the end of a study to see if a given treatment worked. It is a way of measuring whether the primary outcome has been met. An example of a primary endpoint is the number of deaths between the treatment group and the control group. The primary endpoint is decided before the study begins.
Primary Outcome		The outcome of greatest importance (see Outcome Measure).
Primary Therapy		See First-Line Therapy.
Primary Treatment		See First-Line Therapy.
Principal Investigator	PI	If the trial involves more than one hospital, the PI is the designated person at each hospital responsible for the day-to-day running of the clinical trial.
Prognosis		Chance of recovery; a prediction of the outcome of a disease.
Progression		In medicine, the course of a disease, such as cancer, as it becomes worse or spreads in the body.
Progression-Free Survival	PFS	The proportion of people among those treated for cancer whose disease does not worsen at a certain time after trial entry. For example, a progression-free survival rate of 80% at 2 years means that cancer did not grow or spread in four out of five (80%) of the study participants at the two-year time point.
Proliferative Index		A measure of the number of cells in a tumour that are dividing (proliferating).

Term		Definition
Proof Of Concept		An early stage of clinical drug development, when a compound has shown potential for human therapeutic use, after preclinical animal models and early safety testing. This step often links Phase I (first in humans) and dose-ranging Phase II studies.
Proof Of Mechanism (Studies)		Studies that are designed to show that a new medicine reaches its target organ(s), interacts with its molecular target, and affects the biology of the target cells as intended. Phase I clinical studies, or proof of mechanism studies, test the safety of a medicine in humans.
Prospective		In medicine, a study or clinical trial where participants are identified and then followed forward in time.
Prospective Cohort Study		A research study that follows over time groups of individuals who are alike in many ways but differ by a certain characteristic (for example, female nurses who smoke and those who do not smoke) and compares them for a particular outcome (such as lung cancer).
Prostate Screening Antigen	PSA	PSA is a protein made only by the prostate gland. A PSA blood test helps detect prostate cancer. The test measures the level of prostate-specific antigen (PSA) in the blood, but it is not perfect and will not detect all prostate cancers.
Proteins		Proteins are large, complex molecules that play many critical roles in the body. They do most of the work in cells and are required for the structure, function, and regulation of the body's tissues and organs.
Protocol		A document that describes the objective(s), design, methodology, statistical considerations and organisation of a trial.
Protocol Development Group	PDG	The team of people with expertise in the area being researched, such as doctors, researchers and statisticians who help to write the protocol for the trial.

Term			Definition
Proton Beam Therapy	PBT		Proton beam therapy is a type of radiotherapy that uses a beam of high-energy protons, which are small parts of atoms, rather than high-energy X-rays (photons) to treat specific types of cancer.
Proton Magnetic Resonance Spectroscopic Imaging.	PMRSI		See Magnetic Resonance Spectroscopic Imaging.
Pseudonymised			The processing of personal data so that an individual cannot be identified from this data alone.
Public Participation Involvement and Engagement	PPIE		Public Participation Involvement and Engagement is where members of the public: • participate passively in research by having research done to, about or for them (Participation) • advocate actively in research, by working alongside researchers throughout any and all stages of the research trial process (Involvement) • collaborate with researchers to raise awareness and share the results of research with the public (Engagement)
P-value			A term in statistics. It helps show whether a difference found between groups that are being compared is due to chance. A small p-value usually means that the difference between groups is not due to chance alone, but is due to some other factor, such as a treatment one of the groups received. A large p-value usually means that the difference between groups is probably due to chance alone.

Q

Term		Definition
Qualified Person	QP	All manufacturing activities will need to be conducted in a unit which has an Investigation Medicinal Product (IMP) manufacturing authorisation with a named Qualified Person (QP). This person ensures that an IMP batch is only released if there is documentation to confirm compliance with good manufacturing practice (or equivalent).
Qualitative Research		Qualitative research is used to explore and understand people's beliefs, experiences, attitudes, or behaviours. It asks questions about how and why. For example, qualitative research might ask questions about why people want to stop smoking, but it would not ask how many people have tried to stop smoking. This research does not collect data in the form of numbers but might collect data in the form of interview transcripts or notes from focus groups.
Quality Assurance	QA	A process that looks at activities or products on a regular basis to make sure they are being done at the required level of excellence. In clinical trials, QA makes sure that all parts of the trial follow both the law and good clinical practice guidelines.
Quality Control	QC	The steps taken during a trial to ensure that it meets protocol and procedural requirements and is reproducible.

Term		Definition
Quality of Life	QoL	Clinical trials may assess the effect of treatment on a patient's well-being and ability to function in daily life.
		These are measured using QoL tools (questionnaires) which have been developed sometimes by particular cancer types to assess specific aspects of QoL for each condition.
		Some trials now include Patient Reported Outcomes (PROs) as one of the ways to measure QoL.
		These measures are particularly important for patients as they show the impact of the treatment on everyday life.
Quantitative Research		Quantitative research is used to explore and analyse relationships between treatments, interventions, or a person's traits, and a health outcome of interest.
		It captures these relationships with numerical results and figures. For example, quantitative research might ask questions about the most effective ways to stop smoking e.g., what percentage of people that try to quit smoking through the NHS are successful?
		This type of research collects data in the form of numbers (e.g., measurements), categories and dates. The data is often collected by an investigator or supplied by a participant.

R

Term			Definition
Radiation			Energy released in the form of particle or electromagnetic waves. Common sources of radiation include radon gas, cosmic rays from outer space, medical X-rays, and energy given off by a radioisotope (an unstable form of a chemical element that releases radiation as it breaks down and becomes more stable). Radiation can damage cells. It is used to diagnose and treat some types of cancer.
Radiation Therapy			The use of high-energy X-rays or other particles to destroy cancer cells. The most common type of radiation treatment is called external beam radiation therapy, which is given from a machine outside the body.
Radioactive Drug			A drug that contains a radioactive substance and is used to diagnose or treat diseases, including cancer. Also called radiopharmaceutical.
Radioactive Liquid Therapy	RLT		Radioactive liquid therapy is used for some types of cancer. You might have them as a drink, capsules or as an injection.
Radioactive Seed			A small, radioactive pellet that is placed in or near a tumour. Cancer cells are killed by the energy given off as the radioactive material breaks down and becomes more stable.
Radioactive Tracer			A radioactive tracer, radiotracer, or radioactive label is a synthetic derivative of a natural compound in which one or more atoms have been replaced by a radionuclide.

Term		Definition
Radiofrequency Ablation	RFA	Radiofrequency ablation is a minimally invasive technique that shrinks the size of tumours, nodules or other growths in the body. RFA is used to treat a range of conditions, including benign and malignant tumours.
Radiography		A procedure that uses a type of high-energy radiation called X-rays to take pictures of areas inside the body. X-rays pass through the body onto film or a computer, where the pictures are made. The tissues and organs usually appear in various shades of black and white because different tissues allow different amounts of the x-ray beams to pass through them. Radiography is used to help diagnose disease and plan treatment. Also called x-ray imaging.
Radio Imaging		A method that uses radioactive substances to make pictures of areas inside the body. The radioactive substance is injected into the body and locates and binds to specific cells or tissues, including cancer cells. Images are made using a special machine that detects the radioactive substance. Also called a nuclear medicine scan.
Radio-immunoconjugate		A radioactive substance that carries radiation directly to cancer cells. A radioimmunoconjugate is made by attaching a radioactive molecule to an immune substance, such as a monoclonal antibody, that can bind to cancer cells. This may help kill cancer cells without harming normal cells. Radioimmunoconjugates may also be used with imaging to help find cancer cells in the body.

Term		Definition
Radio Immuno-diagnostics		The use of radiolabelled monoclonal antibodies to help diagnose diseases, including cancer. The radiolabelled monoclonal antibody locates and binds to substances in the body, including cancer cells. Images are made using a special machine that detects the radioactive monoclonal antibody.
Radio Immuno-guided Surgery		A procedure that uses radioactive substances to locate tumours so that they can be removed by surgery.
Radio Immuno-therapeutics		The use of radiolabelled monoclonal antibodies to treat diseases, including cancer. The radiolabelled monoclonal antibody locates and binds to substances in the body, including cancer cells. Radiation given off by the radioisotope may help kill the cancer cells.
Radio-immunotherapy		A type of radiation therapy in which a radioactive substance is linked to a monoclonal antibody and injected into the body. The monoclonal antibody can bind to substances in the body, including cancer cells. The radioactive substance gives off radiation, which may help kill cancer cells. Radioimmunotherapy is being used to treat some types of cancer.
Radiology		The use of radiation (such as X-rays) or other imaging technologies (such as ultrasound and magnetic resonance imaging) to diagnose or treat disease.

Term	Definition
Radiology Report	A detailed report that describes the results of an imaging test. A radiology report includes information about the type of imaging test that was done and how it was done. It also includes a brief medical history of the person having the test, including any symptoms or known diseases and why the test was needed. The report also describes the findings seen in the areas of the body that were scanned and compares them with findings from a previous imaging test, if available. A summary of all the findings, which may be used to make a diagnosis of a disease, and any recommendations for further testing are also included in the report.
Radionuclide Scanning	A procedure that produces scans of structures inside the body, including areas where there are cancer cells. Radionuclide scanning is used to diagnose, stage, and monitor disease. A small amount of a radioactive chemical (radionuclide) is injected into a vein or swallowed. Different radionuclides then travel through the blood to different organs. A machine with a special camera moves over the person lying on a table and detects the type of radiation given off by the radionuclides. A computer forms an image of the areas where the radionuclide builds up. These areas may contain cancer cells. Also called Scintigraphy.
Radiopharmaceuticals	Radiopharmaceuticals (also known as medicinal radio compounds) are a group of pharmaceutical drugs containing radioactive isotopes. Radiopharmaceuticals can be used as both diagnostic and therapeutic agents.

Term		Definition
Radiotherapy (4D)	4DRT	The explicit inclusion of changes in anatomy overtime during the imaging, planning, and delivery of radiotherapy.
Radio Wave		A type of wave made when an electric field and a magnetic field are combined. Radio waves are being studied in the treatment of several types of cancer and other conditions. The radio waves are sent through needles inserted into tumour tissue and may kill cancer cells. Radio waves are also used in MRI to create detailed images of areas inside the body.
Random Allocation		When the treatment given to trial participants is chosen at random. This means that the participant or investigator cannot influence which treatment is given.
Randomisation		See Randomised Controlled Trial.
Randomised Allocation		See Randomised Controlled Trial.
Randomised Controlled Trial	RCT	A trial where participants are randomly allocated to either an experimental or control treatment to ensure that each group of patients are as similar as possible. By randomly assigning patients to the treatment or control group, any differences seen in the groups at the end of the trial can be attributed to the difference in treatment alone and not to differences in the groups caused by bias. Also called Randomisation or Randomised Allocation.
Real-World Data	RWD	Data relating to a patient's health or the delivery of healthcare, collected outside of a controlled trial. This can be routinely collected from electronic health records (hospitals, medical practices) or patient registries.

Term		Definition
Red Blood Cell		A type of blood cell that is made in the bone marrow and found in the blood. Red blood cells contain a protein called haemoglobin, which carries oxygen from the lungs to all parts of the body. Checking the number of red blood cells in the blood is usually part of a complete blood cell (CBC) test. It may be used to look for conditions such as anaemia, dehydration, malnutrition, and leukaemia. Also called erythrocyte.
Reduced Penetrance		See Incomplete Penetrance.
Refractory Cancer		Cancer that does not respond to treatment. The cancer may be resistant at the beginning of treatment or it may become resistant during treatment. Also called resistant cancer.
Regimen		A treatment plan that includes expected treatments and procedures, medications and their doses, the schedule of treatments, and how long the treatment will last.
Regional Hyperthermia		In regional hyperthermia, a part of the body, such as an organ, limb, or body cavity (a hollow space within the body) is heated. It is not hot enough to destroy the cancer cells outright. It is usually combined with chemotherapy or radiation therapy.
Relative Odds		See Odds Ratio.

Term			Definition
Relative Risk			Compares the risk of disease between two groups of people. In cancer research, relative risk is used in prospective (forward-looking) studies, such as cohort studies and clinical trials. A relative risk of one means there is no difference between two groups in terms of their risk of cancer, based on whether or not they were exposed to a certain substance or factor, or how they responded to two treatments being compared. A relative risk of greater than one or of less than one usually means that being exposed to a certain substance or factor either increases (relative risk greater than one) or decreases (relative risk less than one) the risk of cancer, or that the treatments being compared do not have the same effects. Also called the risk ratio.
Relative Survival			Compares the proportion of people surviving between those with a certain disease and those without.
Remission			The disappearance of the signs and symptoms of cancer but not necessarily the entire disease. The disappearance can be temporary or permanent.
Remission Induction Therapy			Initial treatment with anti-cancer drugs to decrease the signs or symptoms of cancer or make them disappear.
Research			A study designed and conducted to generate new knowledge.
Research and Development	R&D		The testing of a drug or procedure in humans to determine its safety and effectiveness.
Research Base			Refers to the institutions, clinical staff, and patients that can take part in a clinical trial.

Term			Definition
Research Design Service	RDS		A network in England to help researchers develop and design high-quality research proposals for submission to national, peer-reviewed funding competitions for applied health or social care research.
Researcher			Someone conducting a study or trial.
Research Ethics Committee	REC		Research Ethics Committees review research applications and give an opinion about whether the research is ethical. RECs are independent of the research sponsors (the organisation responsible for the management of the research), funders and investigators.
Research Governance Framework	RGF		A set of standards and principles for carrying out health-related or social/community care research in the UK. It is mandatory for all research taking place in the NHS and using NHS resources. It aims to improve research and safeguard the public by: • enhancing ethical awareness and scientific quality • promoting good practice • reducing adverse incidents and ensuring lessons are learned • forestalling poor performance and misconduct.
Research Passport			A mechanism for assuring NHS organisations of the pre-engagement checks conducted on a researcher; and other SOPs for handling the HR arrangements for researchers.

Term	Definition
Research Study	A scientific study of nature that sometimes includes processes involved in health and disease. For example, clinical trials are research studies that involve people. These studies may be related to new ways to screen, prevent, diagnose, and treat disease. They may also study certain outcomes and certain groups of people by looking at data collected in the past or future.
Resection	Removal of a tumour during cancer surgery. Also called an excision.
Residual Disease	Cancer cells that remain after attempts to remove the cancer have been made.
Resistant Cancer	See Refractory Cancer.
Response rate	The percentage of patients whose cancer shrinks or disappears after treatment.
Restaging	A process used to find out the amount or spread of cancer in the body if it comes back or gets worse after treatment. Restaging may also be carried out to find out how the cancer responded to treatment. If restaging is done and a new stage is assigned, the new stage will be marked with an 'r' in front of it to show that it's different from the original stage. Usually, the original stage stays the same, even if the cancer comes back or gets worse. The same tests that were done to diagnose the cancer are usually done again. Restaging helps doctors plan the best treatment for cancer that has come back or gotten worse.
Retrospective Cohort Study	See Historic Cohort Study.
Retrospective Study	See Case-control Study.

Term		Definition
Ribonucleic Acid	RNA	One of two types of nucleic acid made by cells. RNA contains information that has been copied from DNA (the other type of nucleic acid). Cells make several different forms of RNA, and each form has a specific job in the cell. Many forms of RNA have functions related to making proteins. RNA is also the genetic material of some viruses instead of DNA. RNA can be made in the laboratory and used in research studies.
Risk Assessment		A process used to estimate the risk that a certain event will happen. In medicine, this may include a person's risk of having a child with a certain condition or disease, such as cancer. It may also be used to estimate the risk of carrying a certain gene mutation (change), or of having an adverse event (unexpected medical problem) in response to certain types of drugs or other substances. A risk assessment may be done by collecting information about a person's age, sex, personal and family medical history, ethnic background, lifestyle, and other factors and using statistical tools to calculate risk.
Risk-Benefit Ratio		The risk to individual participants versus the potential benefit. The risk-benefit ratio may differ depending on the condition being treated.
Risk Factor		Something that increases the chance of developing a disease. Some examples of risk factors for cancer are age, a family history of certain cancers, use of tobacco products, being exposed to radiation or certain chemicals, infection with certain viruses or bacteria, and certain genetic changes.

Term		Definition
Risk Group		In medicine, risk groups are used to describe people who are alike in important ways. For example, patients with the same type of cancer may be divided into different risk groups that depend on certain aspects of their disease. These risk groups may be based on the patient's chance of being cured (good versus poor) or the chance that their disease will come back (high versus low). Treatment may be based on which risk group a patient falls into. Risk groups can also be used to describe people who share traits and behaviours that affect their chance of developing a disease. For example, people who do not smoke are in a lower risk group for lung cancer than people who smoke.
Risk Model		In medicine, a tool used to estimate a person's risk of developing a certain condition or disease, such as cancer. Risk models may also be used to estimate a person's risk of carrying a certain gene change or of having a child with a certain condition. Risk models use computer programs and statistics to estimate risk based on information about a person that may include their age, sex, personal and family medical history, ethnic background, lifestyle, and other factors. There are many types of risk models, and each model looks at different factors that increase risk in different groups of people.
Risk Ratio		See Relative Risk.
Robotic-assisted Bronchoscopy		Robotic-assisted bronchoscopy allows the physician to precisely place the biopsy needle into different areas of the nodule in real-time. Often, a pathologist is on-site to look at the tissue under the microscope during the procedure and provide feedback on whether enough tissue was sampled.

Term		Definition
Run-In Period		The time before a trial starts when no trial drug is given to participants. During this time, patients may still receive standard treatments for their disease if these treatments are allowed within the trial period.

S

Term		Definition
Safety		In clinical trials, the goal of safety monitoring is to identify, evaluate, minimise and appropriately manage risks.
Safety Monitoring Committee	SMC	A safety monitoring committee is usually set up before a trial starts. The SMC looks at the safety and design of the trial. The committee also meet regularly to check how things are going. These meetings are at particular timepoints that are set out in the protocol.
Sample Size		The number of participants in the trial. The intended sample size is the number of participants planned to be included in the trial, usually determined using a statistical power calculation. This will be based on the clinically significant effects that trial organisers hope to see.
Satellite Tumour		A group of tumour cells in an area near the primary (original) tumour. In melanoma, satellite tumours occur within 2 centimetres of the primary tumour, on or under the skin, and can be seen without a microscope. Satellite tumours may also be found in other types of cancer, including cancers of the breast, lung, liver, and brain. Having a satellite tumour is a sign that the cancer has spread from where it first formed (metastasised).

Term		Definition
Scan		A type of test that takes detailed pictures of areas inside the body. A scan may also refer to the picture that gets made during the test. Scans may be used to help diagnose disease, plan treatment, or find out how well treatment is working. There are many different types of scans, including: • computed tomography (CT) scans which are carried out using an x-ray machine linked to a computer. • magnetic resonance imaging (MRI) scans, which are carried out using radio waves and a powerful magnet linked to a computer. • nuclear medicine scans (such as bone scans and liver scans), which are carried out using small amounts of radioactive substances that are injected into the body and a special machine to detect the radioactive substance.
Scatter radiation		Radiation that spreads out in different directions from a radiation beam when the beam interacts with a substance, such as body tissue. For example, during x-ray mammography, very small amounts of radiation may be scattered to areas away from the breast, such as the head and neck, sternum, and thyroid gland. The energy of scatter radiation is usually much lower than that of the original radiation beam.
Scintigraphy		See Radionuclide Scanning.
Screening		The process of checking whether a person has a disease or has an increased chance of developing a disease when the person has no symptoms.

Term		Definition
Secondary Cancer		A term used to describe cancer that has spread (metastasised) from the place where it first started to another part of the body. Secondary (metastatic) cancer is the same type of cancer as the primary tumour but has spread to other parts of the body. For example, breast cancer cells that spread to the liver are still breast cancer cells. Also called a secondary tumour.
Secondary Endpoints		The results that are measured at the end of a study, in addition to the main result (primary endpoint), to see if a given treatment worked, and to explore other aspects of the treatment.
Secondary Genomic Finding		A genomic variant, found through the analysis of a person's genome, that is of potential medical value yet is unrelated to the initial reason for examining the person's genome. In certain cases, a secondary genomic finding might offer clinicians the chance to identify a previously unrecognised risk for a disease that could change the medical management of that patient and potentially prevent or more effectively treat the disease.
Secondary Outcome		An outcome used to evaluate the extra effects of an intervention viewed as being less important than the primary outcomes.
Secondary Tumour		See Secondary Cancer.
Second-line Therapy		Treatment that is given when initial treatment (first-line therapy) does not work or stops working.
Second-look Surgery		Surgery performed after primary treatment to determine whether tumour cells remain.

Term		Definition
Second Opinion		In medicine, the opinion of a doctor other than the patient's current doctor.
		The second doctor reviews the patient's medical records and gives an opinion about the patient's health problem and how it should be treated.
		A second opinion may confirm or question the first doctor's diagnosis and treatment plan, give more information about the patient's disease or condition, and offer other treatment options.
Second Primary Cancer		A term used to describe a new primary cancer that occurs in a person who has had cancer in the past.
		Second primary cancers may occur months or years after the original (primary) cancer was diagnosed and treated.
		Certain types of cancer treatment, such as chemotherapy and radiation therapy, may increase the risk of a second primary cancer.
		Having certain inherited gene mutations (changes) and being exposed to certain cancer-causing substances, such as tobacco smoke, may also increase the risk of a second primary cancer.
Selection Bias		An error in choosing the individuals or groups to take part in a study.
		Ideally, the subjects in a study should be very similar to one another and to the larger population from which they are drawn. For example, all individuals with the same disease or condition.
		If there are important differences, the results of the study may not be valid.

Term		Definition
Self-evident Corrections		A list of corrections to the case report form that can be made by the sponsor's data management staff without the requirement for a case-by-case referral to the investigator.
		For example, if a case report form page lists concomitant medications taken by a patient but the box stating, 'Are there any medications this cycle?' is blank, the box may be ticked by the data manager.
		A list of such data correction conventions should be agreed upon by the investigator prior to data management activities taking place.
Sensitivity		In medicine, sensitivity describes how well a test can detect a specific disease or condition in people who actually have the disease or condition.
		No test has 100% sensitivity because some people who have the disease or condition will not be identified by the test (false negative test result).
		Sensitivity may also refer to the way the body reacts to the environment or to drugs, chemicals, or other substances. For example, a person who is sensitive to the sun may have skin that burns easily or get a rash when exposed to the sun.
Sensor		A device that responds to a stimulus, such as heat, light, or pressure, and generates a signal that can be measured or interpreted.
Serious Adverse Event	SAE	A serious adverse event occurs if it is thought that the event is an unwanted serious adverse reaction to the trial medicine.
		However, medical events that are not life-threatening, do not result in death, or do not require hospitalisation may still be considered serious adverse events if they put the participant in danger or require medical or surgical intervention to prevent one of the results listed.

Term		Definition
Serious Adverse Reaction	SAR	A serious adverse reaction is one that either: • results in death, • is life-threatening, • requires inpatient hospitalisation or extends a current hospital stay, • results in an ongoing or significant incapacity or disability, or • causes a congenital anomaly or birth defect.
Serious Breach of Protocol	SBP	A 'serious breach' is a breach which is likely to affect to a significant degree: • the safety or physical or mental integrity of the subjects of the trial, or • the scientific value of the trial.
Serology		The examination of antibodies and other substances in the serum (clear liquid part of the blood). Serology tests are used to look for the presence of antibodies in the blood that show whether a person has been exposed to a virus or other infectious agent.
Serotype		Describes a way of grouping cells or microorganisms, such as bacteria or viruses, based on the antigens or other molecules found on their surfaces. For example, human papillomaviruses (HPVs) are a group of many related viruses, and each virus in the group has its own serotype. The serotypes can cause the viruses to behave differently when they infect people. For example, some HPV serotypes can cause benign (not cancerous) tissue growth, such as warts, whilst others can cause certain types of cancer.
Service Evaluation		A study designed to answer the question 'What standard does this service achieve?'

Term		Definition
Service Level Agreement	SLA	A communication document that makes clear what the supplier will deliver and what the organisation will ensure. It is based on the conditions of contract and specification and does not in any way replace them.
Sestamibi Scan		An imaging test used to find overactive parathyroid glands (four pea-sized glands found on the thyroid) and breast cancer cells, and to diagnose heart disease. The patient receives an injection of a small amount of a radioactive substance called technetium which is bound to another substance called sestamibi. This substance collects in overactive glands, cancer cells, heart muscle, or other tissues and a picture is taken by a gamma camera (a special camera that detects radioactivity).
Sézary cell		A cancerous T-cell (a type of white blood cell) found in the blood, skin, and lymph nodes of patients who have a fast-growing type of skin lymphoma called Sézary syndrome. Under a microscope, Sézary cells have an abnormally shaped nucleus and look larger than normal T-cells.

Term		Definition
Shared Decision-Making	SDM	In medicine, a process whereby the patient, their family, carer and health care professionals work together to decide the best plan of care for the patient. When making a shared decision, the patient's values, goals, and concerns are considered. Shared decision-making helps patients learn more about their health condition, the different testing and treatment options that may be available, and the possible risks and benefits of each option. It is often used when important medical decisions need to be made, such as having a genetic test or cancer screening test, having major surgery, or taking a medicine over a long time.
Shave Biopsy		A procedure in which a skin abnormality and a thin layer of surrounding skin are removed with a small blade for examination under a microscope. Stitches are not needed with this procedure.
Short-term Side Effect		A problem that is caused by treatment of a disease but usually goes away after treatment ends. Short-term side effects of cancer treatment include nausea, vomiting, diarrhoea, hair loss, fatigue, and mouth sores.
Side Effect		An effect of a drug or other type of treatment that is in addition to or beyond its desired effect. Side effects can be harmful or beneficial, and most go away on their own over time. Others may last beyond treatment or appear long after treatment has ended. Some common side effects of cancer treatment are nausea, vomiting, fatigue, pain, decreased blood cell counts, hair loss, and mouth sores.

Term		Definition
Sign		In medicine, a sign is something found during a physical exam or as a result of a laboratory or imaging test that shows that a person may have a condition or disease. Signs can be observed by a healthcare provider or another person. Some examples of signs are fever, swelling, skin rash, high blood pressure, and high blood glucose.
Signalling Pathway		A series of chemical reactions in which a group of molecules in a cell work together to control a cell function, such as cell division or cell death.
Signal Transduction		The process by which a cell responds to substances outside the cell through signalling molecules found on the surface of and inside the cell. Also called cell signalling.
Signal Transduction Inhibitor	STI	A substance that blocks signals passed from one molecule to another inside a cell. Blocking these signals can affect many functions of the cell, including cell division and cell death, and may kill cancer cells. Certain signal transduction inhibitors are being studied in the treatment of cancer.
Signature Molecule		See Biomarker.
Simulation		In cancer treatment, a process used to plan radiation therapy so that the target area is precisely located and marked.
Single-Blind Study		A trial where participants included in the trial do not know which treatment they are given but the investigator does.
Single Nucleotide Polymorphism	SNP	The most common type of change in DNA (molecules inside cells that carry genetic information). SNPs occur when a single nucleotide (building block of DNA) is replaced with another. These changes may cause disease and may affect how a person reacts to bacteria, viruses, drugs, and other substances.

Term		Definition
Single-photon Emission Computed Tomography	SPECT	Single-photon emission computed tomography is a nuclear medicine tomographic imaging technique using gamma rays. SPECT is very similar to conventional nuclear medicine planar imaging using a gamma camera but is able to provide true 3-D information.
Site-Specific Assessment	SSA	Any hospital that wants to take part in a trial has to get approval from their NHS Research and Development department by carrying out an SSA.
Skin Test		A test for an immune response to a compound by placing it on or under the skin.
Small-molecule Drug		A drug that can enter cells easily because it has a low molecular weight. Once inside the cells, it can affect other molecules, such as proteins, and may cause cancer cells to die. This is different to drugs that have a large molecular weight, which keeps them from getting inside cells easily. Many targeted therapies are small-molecule drugs.
Social Determinants Of Health	SDOH	The social, economic, and physical conditions in the places where people are born and where they live, learn, work, play, and get older that can affect their health, well-being, and quality of life. SDOH includes factors such as education level, income, employment, housing, transportation, and access to healthy food, clean air and water, and health care services. SDOH has an important effect on health outcomes, especially in certain groups of people. For example, people who cannot afford healthy food or who do not live in a safe area for exercise are more likely to have a poor diet, be physically inactive, and have obesity. This can increase their risk of developing certain diseases, such as cancer.

Term		Definition
Socio-Economic Status	SES	A way of describing people based on their education, income, and type of job. SES is usually described as low, medium, and high. People with a lower SES usually have less access to financial, educational, social, and health resources than those with a higher SES. As a result, they are more likely to be in poor health and have chronic health conditions and disabilities.
Solid Tumour		An abnormal mass of tissue that usually does not contain cysts or liquid areas. Solid tumours may be benign (not cancer) or malignant (cancer). Different types of solid tumours are named for the type of cells that form them. Examples of solid tumours are sarcomas, carcinomas, and lymphomas. Leukaemia (cancer of the blood) generally does not form solid tumours.
Somatic Therapy	SE	A form of alternative therapy aimed at treating trauma and stress-related disorders, such as PTSD. The primary goal of SE is to modify the trauma-related stress response through bottom-up processing.
Somatostatin Receptor Scintigraphy	SRS	A type of radionuclide scan used to find carcinoid and other types of tumours. Radioactive octreotide, a drug similar to somatostatin, is injected into a vein and travels through the bloodstream. The radioactive octreotide attaches to tumour cells that have receptors for somatostatin. A radiation-measuring device detects the radioactive octreotide and makes pictures showing where the tumour cells are in the body. Also called an octreotide scan.

Term		Definition
Sonogram		A computer picture of areas inside the body created by high-energy sound waves.
		The sound waves bounce off internal tissues or organs and make echoes.
		The echoes form a picture of the body tissues on a computer screen.
		A sonogram may be used to help diagnose diseases, such as cancer.
		Also called an ultrasonogram.
Source data		All information in original records and certified copies of original records of clinical findings, observations, or other activities in a clinical trial necessary for the reconstruction and evaluation of the trial.
		Source data are contained in source documents (original records or certified copies).
		Source data may be in hard copy or electronic format.
Source Documents		Original documents, data, and records.
		For example hospital records, clinical and office charts, laboratory notes, memoranda, subjects' diaries or evaluation checklists, pharmacy dispensing records, recorded data from automated instruments, copies or transcriptions certified after verification as being accurate copies, microfiches, photographic negatives, microfilm or magnetic media, X-rays, subject files, and records kept at the pharmacy, at the laboratories and at medico-technical departments involved in the clinical trial.
Specific Immune Cell		An immune cell such as a T or B-lymphocyte that responds to a single, specific antigen.
Specificity		A measure of a diagnostic test's ability to correctly identify people who do not have the disease.
		No test is 100% specific because some people who do not have the disease will test positive for it (false positive).

Term		Definition
Sponsor		The trial sponsor is legally responsible for ensuring that there are proper arrangements in place to plan and manage the clinical trial.
Sporadic Cancer		Cancer that occurs in people who do not have a family history of that cancer or an inherited change in their DNA that would increase their risk for that cancer.
Spiral CT Scan		See Helical Computed Tomography.
Stable Disease		Cancer that is neither decreasing nor increasing in extent or severity.
Staging		A way of describing cancer, such as where it is located, whether or where it has spread, and whether it is affecting the functions of other organs in the body.
Standard of Care	SOC	The currently accepted best-practice treatment for a disease or condition.
Standard Operating Procedure	SOP	A procedure that describes the activities necessary to complete a task in accordance with industry regulations, laws or even just local standards for running a business.
Statistical Analysis		Statistical analysis uses a set of mathematical rules to analyse numerical and categorical data. It can help researchers decide what data means. For example, statistical analysis can assess whether any difference seen between two groups of people (for example between the groups of people in a clinical trial) is likely to be a reliable finding or simply due to chance.
Statistical Analysis Plan		A document that contains a more technical and detailed elaboration of the principal features of the analysis described in the protocol It includes detailed procedures for executing the statistical analysis of the primary and secondary variables and other data.

Term		Definition
Statistical Significance		Results are said to be statistically significant if the trial data has answered the research question of interest with enough certainty. Statistically significant results often describe a reliable difference between two treatment groups.
Stem Cell		Stem cells are cells with the potential to develop into many different types of cells in the body. They serve as a repair system for the body. There are two main types of stem cells: embryonic stem cells and adult stem cells.
Stem Cell Factor	SCF	A substance that causes blood stem cells (cells from which other types of cells develop) to change into different types of blood cells and increases the number and actions of these cells in the blood.
Stereotactic Ablative Body Radiotherapy	SABR	SABR gives radiotherapy from different angles around the body with the beams meeting at the tumour. The tumour receives a high dose of radiation and the tissues around it receive a much lower dose thus lowering the risk of side effects.
Stereotactic External Beam Radiation Therapy	SBRT	A type of external radiation therapy that uses special equipment to position the patient and precisely deliver radiation to a tumour. The total dose of radiation is divided into several smaller doses given over several days. Stereotactic external beam radiation therapy is used to treat brain tumours and other brain disorders. It is also being studied in the treatment of other types of cancer, such as lung cancer. Also called stereotactic radiation therapy and stereotaxic radiation therapy.
Stereotactic Injection		A procedure in which a computer and a 3-D scanning device are used to inject anti-cancer drugs directly into a tumour.

Term		Definition
Stereotactic Procedure		A procedure that uses special equipment and imaging techniques to find an abnormal area in the brain, breast, lung, or liver and help guide the removal of a tissue sample from that area. Stereotactic procedures are also used to treat some cancers, including cancers of the brain, breast, lung, and liver, by precisely delivering radiation directly to a tumour.
Stereotactic Radiation Therapy		See Stereotactic External Beam Radiation Therapy.
Stereotaxic Radiation Therapy		See Stereotactic External Beam Radiation Therapy.
Stopping Rules		A set of criteria that specify when a participant's, and/or cohort's trial treatment should be stopped. They are usually based on the occurrence and number of severe and serious adverse events or if insufficient treatment benefit is found in interim analyses.
Stratification		Stratification is a way of grouping subsets of patients and is used in randomised trials when factors that can influence the treatment's success are known. For example, participants whose cancer has spread from the original tumour site can be separated (or stratified) from those whose cancer has not spread, since it might be expected that these patients could respond differently to treatment. Evaluating results within different groups allows researchers to assess the impact of treatment without differences in stratification factors influencing results.
Study Agent		A medicine, vitamin, mineral, food supplement, or a combination of them that is being tested in a clinical trial.
Study Completed Date		The date that the last trial participant made the last visit to the study location, and the last samples were collected or last tests performed.

Term	Definition
Study Group	See Control Arm.
Sub-group Analysis	An analysis where the intervention effect is assessed in a specific subset of the participants in a trial, such as those of a certain sex or age.
Subject	See Participant.
Subjective Improvement	In medicine, a term that describes an improvement in a patient's health or well-being based on what is reported by the patient and not what is measured or observed by a healthcare provider. For example, subjective improvement is when a patient says they feel better.
Subset Analysis	In a clinical study, the evaluation of results for some but not all of the patients who participated. The selected patients have one or more characteristics in common, for example, the same stage of disease or the same hormone receptor status.
Substantial Amendment	A change to the terms of the approval given by either the MHRA (in the UK) or the Research Ethics Committee, or a change to the protocol or any other document submitted with the applications which significantly affects one of the following: • the safety or physical or mental integrity of study participants, • the conduct or management of the study, • the scientific value of the study, or • the quality or safety of any investigational medicinal product used in the study.
Sub-Study	A sub-study is a study performed on a sub-group of the patients included in the main clinical trial.

Term		Definition
Summary of Product Characteristics	SPC	The basis of information for health professionals on how to use the medicinal product safely and effectively. They are written and updated by pharmaceutical companies and are based on their research and product knowledge. It is then checked and approved by the UK or European medicines licensing agency. The leaflet that is included in the pack with medicine is a patient-friendly version of this document.
Super-fractionated Radiation Therapy		Radiation treatment in which the total dose of radiation is divided into small doses and treatments are given more than once a day. Super-fractionated radiation therapy is given over the same period of time (days or weeks) as standard radiation therapy. Also called hyper-fractionated radiation therapy.
Suppressor of Fused Homolog gene	SUFU gene	A gene that is part of a cell signalling pathway involved in the formation of tissues and organs, cell growth, and cell division during embryonic development. Mutations (changes) in the SUFU gene may cause cells to grow and divide too quickly or in an uncontrolled way. This may cause abnormal cells, including cancer cells, to grow. SUFU gene mutations have been found in an inherited condition called basal cell nevus syndrome and in a type of brain cancer called medulloblastoma. The SUFU gene is a type of tumour suppressor gene.
Suspected Unexpected Serious Adverse Reaction	SUSAR	A SUSAR is where a suspected serious adverse reaction is unexpected. Unexpected means that the adverse reaction does not match the safety information available about the trial medicine.

Term		Definition
Surveillance		In medicine, closely watching a patient's condition but not treating it unless there are changes in test results. Surveillance is also used to find early signs that a disease has come back. It may also be used for a person who has an increased risk of a disease, such as cancer. During surveillance, certain exams and tests are done on a regular schedule. In public health, surveillance may also refer to the ongoing collection of information about a disease, such as cancer, in a certain group of people. The information collected may include where the disease occurs in a population and whether it affects people of a certain gender, age, or ethnic group.
Survival Rate		The percentage of people in a study or treatment group who are still alive for a certain period of time after they were diagnosed with or started treatment for a disease, such as cancer. The survival rate is often stated as a five-year survival rate, which is the percentage of people in a study or treatment group who are alive five years after their diagnosis or the start of treatment. Also called the overall survival rate.
Susceptibility Gene Mutation		See Predisposing Mutation.
Symptom		Something that a person feels or experiences that may indicate that they have a disease or condition. Symptoms can only be reported by the person experiencing them. They cannot be observed by a health care provider or other person and do not show up on medical tests. For example, symptoms include pain, nausea, fatigue, and anxiety.

Term		Definition
Symptom Management		Care given to help relieve the symptoms of a disease, such as cancer, and the side effects caused by treatment of the disease. Symptom management may help a person feel more comfortable, but it does not treat or cure the disease. It may involve taking certain medicines to relieve pain or nausea or using guided imagery or deep breathing exercises to reduce stress or anxiety. Symptom management is one aspect of palliative care and supportive care.
Synergistic		Used in medicine to describe the interaction of two or more drugs whereby their combined effect is greater than the sum of the effects seen when each drug is given independently.
Systematic Review	SR	A systematic review aims to bring together the results of all studies that have been carried out around the world addressing a particular area of research. The method to search for and select relevant studies for the review must be documented before beginning the review. This ensures that the process can be reproduced and reduces bias. The characteristics and findings of the included studies are combined and presented for the review.
Systemic		Affecting the entire body.
Systemic Anti-Cancer Treatment	SACT	SACT is any drug treatment used to control or treat cancer. The drug types may include hormonal therapy, chemotherapy, immunotherapy, targeted therapy, or a combination of these. SACT can be given on its own, before or after surgery or with radiotherapy.

Term		Definition
Systemic Therapy		Systemic therapy refers to any type of cancer treatment that targets the entire body. For example, chemotherapy, the most common form of systemic therapy, circulates throughout the bloodstream to destroy cancerous cells in multiple locations.

T

Term		Definition
3-Tesla Magnetic Resonance Imaging	3-T MRI	A procedure in which radio waves and a powerful magnet linked to a computer are used to make detailed pictures of areas inside the body. These pictures can show the difference between normal and abnormal tissue. Tesla magnetic resonance imaging has a stronger magnet and makes better images of organs and soft tissue than other types of MRI. It is used to make images of the brain, the spine, the soft tissue of joints, and the inside of bones and blood vessels.
Tailored Intervention		The use of communication, drugs, or other types of treatments that are specific for an individual or a group to improve health or change behaviour.
Targeted Radionuclide Therapy		See Molecular Radiation Therapy.
Targeted Therapy		See Molecular Targeted Therapy.
T-cell		T-cells are a type of white blood cell called lymphocytes. They help the immune system fight germs and protect the body from disease. There are two main types: • Cytotoxic T-cells that destroy infected cells • Helper T-cells that send signals to direct other immune cells to fight infection.
T-cell depletion		A type of treatment to destroy T-cells. Elimination of T-cells from a bone marrow graft taken from a donor may reduce the chance of an immune reaction against the recipient's tissues.

Term		Definition
T-cell exhaustion		Describes a condition in which T-cells lose their ability to kill certain cells, such as cancer cells or cells infected with a virus. This can happen when cancer, chronic infection, or other conditions cause the body's immune system to stay active for a long time. Exhausted T-cells have high amounts of immune checkpoint proteins on their surface, which may keep the activity of the T-cells suppressed. In cancer treatment, drugs that target these proteins may be given to allow the T-cells to better kill cancer cells. Learning more about T-cell exhaustion may help in the development of new types of immunotherapy to treat cancer.
T-cell receptor	TCR	A group of proteins found on T-cells. T-cell receptors bind to certain antigens (proteins) found on abnormal cells, cancer cells, cells from other organisms, and cells infected with a virus or another microorganism. This interaction causes the T-cells to attack these cells and helps the body fight infection, cancer, or other diseases.

Term		Definition
T-cell Transfer Therapy		A type of immunotherapy in which T-cells are given to a patient to help the body fight diseases, such as cancer. In cancer therapy, T-cells are usually taken from the patient's own blood or tumour tissue, grown in large numbers in the laboratory, and then given back to the patient to help the immune system fight the cancer. Sometimes, these T-cells are changed in the laboratory to make them better able to target the patient's cancer cells and kill them. Types of T-cell transfer therapy include chimeric antigen receptor T-cell (CAR T-cell) therapy and tumour-infiltrating lymphocyte (TIL) therapy. T-cell transfer therapy that uses T-cells from a donor is being studied in the treatment of some types of cancer and some infections. Also called adoptive cell therapy, adoptive cell transfer, and cellular adoptive immunotherapy.
Technician		A person trained in the techniques (methods) and skills of a profession. For example, a mammogram technician is trained to perform mammograms.
Telehealth		The delivery of health care from a distance using electronic information and technology, such as computers, cameras, videoconferencing, satellites, wireless communications, and the internet. Also called telemedicine.
Telemedicine		See Telehealth.
Telomere		The ends of a chromosome. Each time a cell divides, the telomeres lose a small amount of DNA and become shorter. Over time, the chromosomes become damaged and the cells die. In cancer cells, the telomeres do not get shorter, and may even become longer, as the cells divide.

284

Term		Definition
Terminal Cancer		Cancer that cannot be cured or controlled with treatment and leads to death. A person with terminal cancer may receive treatment to help control pain and other symptoms so they can be as comfortable as possible and have a better quality of life. Also called end-stage cancer.
Theragnostic		A technique in personalised and nuclear medicine where one radioactive drug is used to identify cancerous tumours and a second radioactive drug is used to treat them.
Therapeutic		Having to do with treating disease and helping healing take place.
Therapeutic Confirmatory		A study that confirms how well a new treatment works after it was shown in early-phase clinical trials that it might be beneficial for patients.
Therapeutic Exploratory		A study to evaluate a medicine's effects in a particular condition and to determine its common short-term side effects.
Therapeutic Use		A study to evaluate side effects that were not seen in earlier trials May also study how well a new treatment works over a long period of time.
Therapy		Treatment.
Thermography		In medicine, a procedure in which a heat-sensing infrared camera is used to record the surface heat produced by different parts of the body. Abnormal tissue growth can cause temperature changes, which may show up on the thermogram. Thermography may be used to diagnose breast cancer and other tumours.
Thermotherapy		Treatment of disease using heat.

Term		Definition
Thrombopoietin	TPO	A substance made by the body that helps make blood cells, especially platelets. A form of TPO made in the laboratory is called recombinant human TPO and rHu TPO. TPO is being studied as a way to increase the number of platelets in cancer patients receiving chemotherapy.
Thymine		One of the four nucleotide bases in DNA, with the other three being adenine (A), cytosine (C) and guanine (G). Within a double-stranded DNA molecule, thymine bases on one strand pair with adenine bases on the opposite strand. The sequence of the four nucleotide bases encodes DNA's information.
Time To Progression	TTP	The length of time from the date of diagnosis or the start of treatment for a disease until the disease starts to get worse or spread to other parts of the body. In a clinical trial, measuring the time to progression is one way to see how well a new treatment works.
Tissue		A group or layer of cells that work together to perform a specific function.
Tissue-agnostic Therapy		See Tumour-agnostic Therapy.
Tissue-Engineered Products	TEPs	TEPS are engineered cells or tissues produced to regenerate, repair, or replace a dysfunctional, diseased, or absent human tissue.

Term		Definition
TNM Cancer Staging System		The TNM cancer staging system examines the extent of the tumour (T), the extent of any spread to the lymph nodes (N), and the presence of metastasis (M). The T category describes the size of the original (primary) tumour; the N category describes the spread of cancer to nearby lymph nodes; and the M category tells whether there are distant metastases (spread of cancer to other parts of the body).
Tolerability		In clinical trials, the degree to which symptomatic and non-symptomatic adverse events associated with the product's administration affect the ability or desire of the patient to adhere to the dose or intensity of therapy.
Tomotherapy		A type of therapy in which radiation is aimed at a tumour from many different directions. Before radiation, a 3-D image of the tumour is taken. The patient lies on a table and is moved through a doughnut-shaped machine. The radiation source in the machine rotates around the patient in a spiral pattern. This helps doctors find the highest dose of radiation that can be used to kill tumour cells whilst causing less damage to nearby tissue. Tomotherapy is a type of intensity-modulated radiation therapy. Also called helical tomotherapy.
Topical Chemotherapy		Treatment with anti-cancer drugs in a lotion or cream applied to the skin.

Term		Definition
Total Body Irradiation		A type of radiation therapy that is given to the entire body. Total body irradiation is often used with high-dose anti-cancer drugs to help prepare a patient for a stem cell transplant. It is carried out to kill any cancer cells that are left in the body and helps make room in the patient's bone marrow for new blood stem cells to grow. Total body irradiation may also help prevent the body's immune system from rejecting transplanted stem cells.
Total Skin Electron Beam Radiation Therapy	TSEB Radiation Therapy	A type of radiation therapy using electrons that is directed at the entire surface of the body. This type of radiation goes into the outer layers of the skin but does not go deeper into tissues and organs below the skin.
Trace Element		An element found in very small amounts in a given substance. Organisms need certain trace elements to survive.
Tracer		A substance (such as a radioisotope) used in imaging procedures.
Transcription		The process by which a cell makes an RNA copy of a piece of DNA. This RNA copy, called messenger RNA (mRNA), carries the genetic information needed to make proteins in a cell. It carries the information from the DNA in the nucleus of the cell to the cytoplasm, where proteins are made.
Transcription Factor		One of a group of proteins that play an important role in controlling the activity of genes. Transcription factors help control when and how genes are turned on or off in a cell by binding to nearby DNA and to other DNA-associated proteins.

Term		Definition
Transcriptomics		The study of all RNA molecules in a cell. RNA is copied from pieces of DNA and contains information to make proteins and perform other important functions in the cell. Transcriptomics is used to learn more about how genes are turned on in different types of cells and how this may help cause certain diseases, such as cancer.
Transfer Factor		A substance made by some white blood cells. Transfer factor from one person's white blood cells may be able to cause a specific immune response when injected into the skin of another person.
Transformation		In cancer, the change that a normal cell undergoes as it becomes malignant.
Translation		The process by which a cell makes proteins using the genetic information carried in messenger RNA (mRNA). The mRNA is made by copying DNA, and the information it carries tells the cell how to link amino acids together to form proteins.
Translational Research		The process by which the results of research carried out in the laboratory are used to develop new ways to diagnose and treat disease.
Transoral Robotic Surgery	TORS	Surgery in which a robot with arms is used to remove cancer from hard-to-reach areas of the mouth and throat. Cameras attached to the robot give a 3-D image that a surgeon can see. The surgeon guides tools at the ends of the robot arms to remove the cancer.
Treatment Course		When a treatment cycle is repeated multiple times on a regular schedule, it constitutes a treatment course. A treatment course can last for several months.

Term		Definition
Treatment Cycle		A period of treatment followed by a period of rest (no treatment) that is repeated on a regular schedule. For example, treatment given for one week followed by three weeks of rest is one treatment cycle.
Treatment Field		In radiation therapy, the place on the body where the radiation beam is aimed.
Treatment Group		See Control Arm.
Treatment Plan		A detailed plan with information about a patient's disease, the goal of treatment, the treatment options for the disease and possible side effects, and the expected length of treatment. A treatment plan may also include information about regular follow-up care after treatment ends.
Treatment Schedule		A step-by-step guide to the treatment that a patient is going to receive. A treatment schedule includes the type of treatment that will be given (such as chemotherapy or radiation therapy), how it will be given (such as by mouth or by infusion into a vein), and how often it will be given (such as once a day or once a week). It also includes the amount of time between courses of treatment and the total length of time of treatment.

Term		Definition
Treatment Summary		A detailed summary of a patient's disease, the type of treatment the patient received, and any side effects or other problems caused by treatment. It usually includes results of laboratory tests (such as pathology reports and biomarker tests) and imaging tests (such as X-rays, CT scans, and MRIs), and whether a patient took part in a clinical trial. A treatment summary may be used to help plan follow-up care after treatment for a disease, such as cancer.
Trial Identification Number	Trial ID	Every patient is assigned a unique trial ID when they are enrolled into a trial. This number is used to identify the patient during the treatment and follow-up phase.
Trial Management Group	TMG	A group which monitors a trial to ensure that the protocol is followed and ensures the safety of participants and the quality of the trial. A TMG usually consists of key trial personnel such as the Chief Investigator, the trial manager, a statistician, the Principal Investigators at relevant sites, and patient advocates.
Trial Master File	TMF	The collection of essential documents which allows a clinical trial to be reconstructed and evaluated. It is basically the story of how a trial has been managed.
Trial Participant		An individual whose reactions or responses to certain interventions are evaluated during a clinical trial.
Trial Site		A hospital site where a trial is being conducted.
Trial Sponsor		See Clinical Trial Sponsor.

Term		Definition
Trial Steering Committee	TSC	A group with overall responsibility for a trial. The TSC makes sure that a trial is conducted properly and that the protocol is followed. The TSC is made up of independent experts in the area of research, the Chief Investigator and members of the trial team, and patient advocates.
T-test		A statistical test that is used to find out if there is a real difference between the means (averages) of two different groups. It is sometimes used to see if there is a significant difference in response to treatment between groups in a clinical trial.
Tumour		A mass formed when normal cells begin to change and grow uncontrollably. A tumour can be benign (non-cancerous) or malignant (cancerous). Also called a neoplasm, nodule or mass.
Tumour-agnostic Therapy		A type of therapy that uses drugs or other substances to treat cancer based on the cancer's genetic and molecular features without regard to the cancer type or where the cancer started in the body. Tumour-agnostic therapy uses the same drug to treat all cancer types that have the genetic mutation (change) or biomarker that is targeted by the drug. It is a type of targeted therapy. Also called tissue-agnostic therapy.
Tumour Biopsy		Taking a sample of tissue so that it can be looked at under a microscope. This is the only way to be certain if an abnormal area is cancerous or not. You may also have a biopsy to find out more about the cancer.

Term		Definition
Tumour Board Review		A treatment planning process in which a group of cancer doctors and other health care specialists meet regularly to review and discuss new and complex cancer cases. The goal of a tumour board review is to decide as a group on the best treatment plan for a patient. These meetings can involve specialists from many areas of health care, including medical oncologists, radiation oncologists, surgeons, pathologists, radiologists, genetics experts, nurses, physical therapists, and social workers.
Tumour Burden		The number of cancer cells, the size of a tumour, or the amount of cancer in the body. Also called tumour load.
Tumour Debulking		Surgical removal of as much of a tumour as possible. Tumour debulking may increase the chance that chemotherapy or radiation therapy will kill all the tumour cells. It may also be done to relieve symptoms or help the patient live longer. Also called debulking.
Tumour-derived		Taken from an individual's own tumour tissue. It may be used in the development of a vaccine that enhances the body's ability to build an immune response to the tumour.
Tumour DNA Sequencing		A laboratory method used to learn the exact order (sequence) of the chemical building blocks that make up tumour DNA. Errors in the sequence of the building blocks can cause cancer cells to grow and spread. Knowing the DNA sequence of a person's tumour may help plan treatment that targets the specific error in the tumour.

Term		Definition
Tumour Grade		A description of a tumour based on how abnormal the cancer cells and tissue look under a microscope and how quickly the cancer cells are likely to grow and spread. Low-grade cancer cells look more like normal cells and tend to grow and spread more slowly than high-grade cancer cells. Grading systems are different for each type of cancer. They are used to help plan treatment and determine prognosis. Also called grade and histologic grade.
Tumour-infiltrating Lymphocyte	TIL	A type of immune cell that has moved from the blood into a tumour. TILs can recognise and kill cancer cells. In cancer therapy, TILs are removed from a patient's tumour, grown in large numbers in a laboratory, and then given back to the patient to help the immune system kill the cancer cells.
Tumour-infiltrating Lymphocyte Therapy	TILT	A type of treatment in which tumour-infiltrating lymphocytes are removed from a patient's tumour and grown in large numbers in a laboratory. These lymphocytes are then given back to the patient by infusion to help the immune system kill the cancer cells.
Tumour Initiation		A process in which normal cells are changed so that they are able to form tumours. Substances that cause cancer can be tumour initiators.

Term		Definition
Tumour Marker		A substance found in tissue, blood, bone marrow, or other body fluids that may be a sign of cancer or certain benign (non-cancer) conditions. Most tumour markers are proteins made by both normal cells and cancer cells, but they are made in higher amounts by cancer cells. Genetic changes in tumour tissue, such as gene mutations, patterns of gene expression, and other changes in tumour DNA or RNA, are also being used as tumour markers.
Tumour Marker Test		A test that measures the amount of tumour markers in tissue, blood, urine, or other body fluids. A tumour marker test is usually done with other tests, such as biopsies or imaging, to help diagnose some types of cancer. It may also be used to help plan treatment or find out how well treatment is working, give a likely prognosis, or find out if cancer has come back or spread to other parts of the body.
Tumour Micro-environment		The normal cells, molecules, and blood vessels that surround and feed a tumour cell. A tumour can change its micro-environment, and the micro-environment can affect how a tumour grows and spreads.
Tumour Model		Cells, tissues, or animals used to study the development and progression of cancer and to test new treatments before they are given to humans.
Tumour Mutational Burden	TMB	The total number of mutations (changes) found in the DNA of cancer cells. Knowing the tumour mutational burden may help plan the best treatment. For example, tumours that have a high number of mutations appear to be more likely to respond to certain types of immunotherapy. Tumour mutational burden is being used as a type of biomarker.

Term		Definition
Tumour Necrosis Factor	TNF	A protein made by white blood cells in response to an antigen (a substance that causes the immune system to make a specific immune response) or infection. TNF can also be made in the laboratory. It may boost a person's immune response and also may cause necrosis (cell death) of some types of tumour cells. TNF is being studied in the treatment of some types of cancer. It is a type of cytokine.
Tumour Profiling		A laboratory method that checks for the presence of certain genes, proteins, or other molecules in a sample of blood or tumour tissue. Tumour profiling may provide information about certain molecular or genetic changes in a tumour, such as gene mutations or other changes in tumour DNA. It may be used to help plan treatment or predict whether cancer will come back or spread to other parts of the body.
Tumour Volume		The size of a cancer measured by the amount of space taken up by the tumour.

U

Term		Definition
Ultrasonogram		See Sonogram.
Ultrasound		An ultrasound is an imaging test that uses sound waves to make pictures of organs, tissues, and other structures inside the body. It allows the health care provider to see into the body without surgery. Ultrasound is also called ultrasonography or sonography. Ultrasound images may be called sonograms.
Ultrasound Energy		A form of therapy being studied as an anti-cancer treatment. Intensified ultrasound energy can be directed at cancer cells to heat them and kill them.
Ultrasound-guided Biopsy		A biopsy procedure that uses an ultrasound imaging device to find an abnormal area of tissue and guide its removal for examination under a microscope.
Ultraviolet Radiation	UVR	Invisible rays that are part of the energy that comes from the sun. Ultraviolet radiation that reaches the Earth's surface is made up of two types of rays, called UVA and UVB. UVR also comes from sun lamps and tanning beds. In medicine, ultraviolet radiation also comes from special lamps or a laser and is used to treat certain skin conditions such as psoriasis, vitiligo, and skin tumours of cutaneous T-cell lymphoma.

Term		Definition
Umbrella Trial		A type of clinical trial that tests how well new drugs or other substances work in patients who have the same type of cancer but different gene mutations (changes) or biomarkers. In umbrella trials, patients receive treatment based on the specific mutation or biomarker found in their cancer. The drugs being tested may change during the trial, as new targets and drugs are found. Umbrella trials may allow new drugs to be tested and approved more quickly than traditional clinical trials.
Unclassified Variant		See Variant of Uncertain Significance.
Uncontrolled Study		A clinical study that lacks a comparison (control) group.
Unconventional Cancer Treatment		Approaches that use substances or methods of treating cancer that have not been shown to be effective by accepted scientific methods, such as through carefully designed clinical trials.
Undifferentiated		A term used to describe cells or tissues that do not have specialised ('mature') structures or functions. Undifferentiated cancer cells often grow and spread quickly.
Upstaging		In cancer, changing the stage used to describe a patient's cancer from a lower stage (less extensive) to a higher stage (more extensive). Upstaging is based on the results of additional staging tests. It is important to know the stage of the disease in order to plan the best treatment.
Urgent Safety Measure		An appropriate measure required to be taken in order to protect the subjects of a clinical trial against any immediate hazard to their health or safety.

V

Term		Definition
Valid Research Application		A complete NIHR research application that has been received by the NHS provider following its submission via IRAS enables regulatory reviews by other agencies (including but not limited to the Research Ethics Committee and MHRA approval) to be conducted in parallel with the work on NHS permission by the contractor.
Variable		Information collected during a clinical trial. For example, one variable might be 'weight'. This would then be checked at set time points throughout the trial.
Variant		See mutation.
Variant Of Uncertain Significance	VUS	A change in a gene's DNA sequence that has an unknown effect on a person's health. There is usually not enough information about a variant of uncertain significance to know whether it increases a person's risk of developing a disease, such as cancer. Also called an unclassified variant or a variant of unknown significance.
Variant Of Unknown Significance		See Variant Of Uncertain Significance.
Volumetric Modulated Arc Radiotherapy	VMAR	VMAR delivers the radiation dose as the treatment machine rotates. This technique shapes the radiation dose to the tumour. At the same time, it reduces the dose to the organs surrounding the tumour.

W

Term		Definition
Wash-Out Period		The time given for a medicine to leave the body.
Watchful Waiting		Closely watching a patient's condition but not giving any treatment unless signs or symptoms appear or change. Watchful waiting may be used when the risks of treatment or repeated tests, such as biopsies, are greater than the possible benefits. During watchful waiting, certain exams and tests may be done periodically to monitor the condition. Watchful waiting is sometimes used in certain types of prostate cancer. It is a type of expectant management.
Well-differentiated		Cells and tissue that have mature (specialised) structures and functions. In cancer, well-differentiated cancer cells look more like normal cells under a microscope and tend to grow and spread more slowly than poorly differentiated or undifferentiated cancer cells.

Term		Definition
White Blood Cell		A type of blood cell that is made in the bone marrow and found in the blood and lymph tissue.
		White blood cells are part of the body's immune system.
		They help the body fight infection and other diseases.
		Types of white blood cells are:
		• granulocytes (neutrophils, eosinophils, and basophils),
		• monocytes, and
		• lymphocytes (T-cells and B-cells).
		Checking the number of white blood cells in the blood is usually part of a complete blood cell (CBC) test.
		It may be used to look for conditions such as infection, inflammation, allergies, and leukaemia.
		Also called a leukocyte.
Whole-brain Radiation Therapy		See Whole-brain Radiotherapy.
Whole-brain Radiotherapy	WBRT	A type of external radiation therapy used to treat patients who have cancer in the brain.
		It is often used to treat patients whose cancer has spread to the brain, or who have more than one tumour or tumours that cannot be removed by surgery.
		Radiation is given to the whole brain over a period of many weeks.
		Also called whole-brain radiation therapy.

Term		Definition
Whole Exome Sequencing	WES	A laboratory method that is used to learn the exact order of all the building blocks that make up the pieces of a person's DNA that contain information for making proteins. These pieces (exons) are thought to make up about 1% of a person's genome (complete set of DNA). WES is used to find mutations (changes) in genes that may cause diseases, such as cancer.
Whole Genome Sequencing	WGS	A laboratory method that is used to learn the exact order of all of the building blocks (nucleotides) that make up a person's genome (complete set of DNA). It is used to find changes that may cause diseases, such as cancer.
Wild-type gene		A term used to describe a gene when it is found in its natural, non-mutated (unchanged) form. Mutated (changed) forms of certain genes have been found in some types of cancer. Knowing whether a patient's tumour has a wild-type or mutated gene may help plan cancer treatment.
World Health Organisation	WHO	The part of the United Nations responsible for global public health.

X

Term		Definition
X-linked Dominant Inheritance		One of the ways a genetic trait or condition caused by a mutated (changed) gene on the X chromosome can be passed down (inherited) from parent to child. In X-linked dominant inheritance, a genetic condition can occur when the child inherits one copy of a mutated (changed) gene on the X chromosome from one parent. Daughters have a 50% chance of inheriting the mutated X-linked gene from their mother and a 100% chance of inheriting the mutated X-linked gene from their father. Sons have a 50% chance of inheriting the mutated X-linked gene from their mother and a 0% chance of inheriting the mutated X-linked gene from their father.
X-linked Recessive Inheritance		One of the ways a genetic trait or condition caused by a mutated (changed) gene on the X chromosome can be passed down (inherited) from parent to child. In X-linked recessive inheritance, a daughter inherits a single mutated gene on the X chromosome from one of her parents. The X chromosome she inherits from the other parent will usually cancel the effect of the mutation, and she most likely will not have the genetic condition. If she inherits a mutated copy of the gene from both parents, she will be affected by the condition. Fathers cannot pass X-linked recessive conditions to their sons. When a son inherits a mutated gene on the X chromosome from his mother, the genetic condition is more likely to occur. X-linked recessive conditions most often occur in males.

Term	Definition
X-rays	X-rays are used in cancer diagnosis. For example, chest radiographs and mammograms are often used for early cancer detection or to see if cancer has spread to the lungs or other areas in the chest. Mammograms use X-rays to look for tumours or suspicious areas in the breasts.
X-ray Therapy	A type of radiation therapy that uses high-energy radiation from X-rays to kill cancer cells and shrink tumours.

Y

Term	Definition
Yttrium	A metal of the rare-earth group of elements. A radioactive form of yttrium (such as yttrium Y-90) may be attached to a monoclonal antibody or other molecule that can locate and bind to cancer cells and be used to diagnose or treat some types of cancer.

Z

Term		Definition

Useful Resources

Cancer Research UK
Types of Clinical Trials
https://www.cancerresearchuk.org/about-cancer/find-a-clinical-trial/what-clinical-trials-are/types-of-clinical-trials
Cancer Statistics Terminology Explained
https://www.cancerresearchuk.org/health-professional/cancer-statistics/cancer-stats-explained/statistics-terminology-explained
Phases of Clinical Trials
https://www.cancerresearchuk.org/about-cancer/find-a-clinical-trial/what-clinical-trials-are/phases-of-clinical-trials
About Cancer
https://www.cancerresearchuk.org/about-cancer/what-is-cancer#:~:text=A%20primary%20tumour%20is%20the,systems%2C%20and%20the%20hormone%20system
National Institute for Health and Care Excellence (NICE)
Glossary of Terms Used in Research Trials
https://www.nice.org.uk/glossary?letter=a
National Institute for Health and Care Research (NIHR)
Glossary of terms used in research trials
https://www.nihr.ac.uk/glossary
Glossary available from NIHR Clinical Trials Toolkit:
https://www.ct-toolkit.ac.uk/glossary/?letter=A#SKPostAToZ
National Health Service
Glossary of Terms Used in NHS
https://www.england.nhs.uk/get-involved/resources/involvejargon/
National Health Service Health Research Authority (HRA)
Glossary of Terms Used by NHS Research Authority and Research Ethics Committees
https://www.hra.nhs.uk/approvals-amendments/glossary/

Endnotes

[i] https://www.nihr.ac.uk/documents/patient-and-public-involvement-and-engagement-resource-pack/31218 (Accessed 2 April 2024)

[ii] https://www.khanacademy.org/science/biology/principles-of-physiology/body-structure-and-homeostasis/a/tissues-organs-organ-systems#:~:text=The%20body%20has%20levels%20of,organs%20cooperate%20to%20process%20food. (Accessed on 8 February 2024)

[iii] https://theconversation.com/the-human-body-has-37-trillion-cells-if-we-can-work-out-what-they-all-do-the-results-could-revolutionise-healthcare-185654#:~:text=The%20diversity%20of%20human%20cells,proteins%20from%20an%20immune%20cell (Accessed on 31 January 2024)

[iv] https://www.cancer.gov/about-cancer/understanding/what-is-cancer#:~:text=DNA%20repair%20genes%20are%20involved,the%20cells%20to%20become%20cancerous. (Accessed on 8 February 2024)

[v] https://www.verywellhealth.com/t-cells-2252171 (Accessed on 14 January 2024)

[vi] https://www.cancerresearch.org/blog/april-2019/how-does-the-immune-system-work-cancer (Accessed on 14 January 2024)

[vii] Hanahan D, Weinberg RA (Accessed 14 January 2024) 'The hallmarks of cancer,' *Cell,* 2000;100:57–70. doi: 10.1016/S0092-8674(00)81683-9.

[viii] https://www.cancer.gov/types (Accessed on 17 February 2024)

ix https://www.cancer.net/navigating-cancer-care/cancer-basics/cancer-care-team/types-oncologists (Accessed on 24 January 2024)

x https://www.nhs.uk/conditions/breast-cancer/prevention/#:~:text=mastectomy)%20or%20medicine.-,Mastectomy,cancer%20by%20up%20to%2090%25 (Accessed on 24 January 2024)

xi https://www.ncbi.nlm.nih.gov/pmc/articles/PMC2802672/ (Accessed on 24 January 2024)

xii https://news.cancerresearchuk.org/2015/02/04/why-are-cancer-rates-increasing/ (Accessed on 31 January 2024)

xiii https://www.cancerresearchuk.org/about-cancer/find-a-clinical-trial/how-clinical-trials-are-planned-and-organised/how-long-it-takes-for-a-new-drug-to-go-through-clinical-trials (Accessed 30 January 2024)

xiv https://www.cancerresearchuk.org/about-cancer/find-a-clinical-trial/what-clinical-trials-are/types-of-clinical-trials (Accessed on 24 January 2024)

xv https://www.nihr.ac.uk/about-us/who-we-are/ (Accessed on 14 January 2024)

xvi https://www.nihr.ac.uk/news/nihr-announces-nearly-800m-to-turn-research-into-new-treatments/31653 (Accessed on 30 January 2024)

xvii https://www.nihr.ac.uk/news/112-million-investment-in-nihr-clinical-research-facilities-announced/19897 (Accessed on 30 January 2024)

xviii https://www.nihr.ac.uk/explore-nihr/support/clinical-research-network.htm (Accessed on 14 January 2024)

xix https://www.nihr.ac.uk/explore-nihr/support/clinical-research-network.htm (Accessed on 30 January 2024)

xx https://www.nihr.ac.uk/explore-nihr/funding-programmes/invention-for-innovation.htm (Accessed on 14 January 2024)

[xxi] https://www.charitychoice.co.uk/charities/health/cancer (Accessed on 24 January 2024)

[xxii] https://www.cancerresearchuk.org/about-us/our-organisation/how-we-spend-your-money (Accessed on 24 January 2024)

[xxiii] https://news.bms.com/news/details/2020/Bristol-Myers-Squibb-Provides-Update-on-Phase-3-IDHENTIFY-Trial-in-Patients-with-Relapsed-or-Refractory-Acute-Myeloid-Leukemia/default.aspx (Accessed on 24 January 2024)

[xxiv] https://www.nature.com/articles/bjc201677#:~:text=Costs%20in%20the%20year%20of,in%20lung%20cancer%20patients%2C%20respectively (Accessed on 24 January 2024)

[xxv] https://www.cancerresearchuk.org/funding-for-researchers/patient-involvement-toolkit-for-researchers (Accessed on 14 January 2024)

[xxvi] https://clinregs.niaid.nih.gov/country/united-kingdom#:~:text=As%20per%20the%20MHCTR%20and,the%20United%20Kingdom%20(UK) (Accessed on 24 January 2024)

[xxvii] https://www.universitiesuk.ac.uk/topics/research-and-innovation/concordat-support-research-integrity (Accessed on 24 January 2024)

[xxviii] https://www.ema.europa.eu/en/documents/scientific-guideline/ich-e-9-statistical-principles-clinical-trials-step-5_en.pdf (Accessed on 24 January 2024)

[xxix] https://health.ec.europa.eu/latest-updates/good-lay-summary-practice-guidance-2021-10-04_en (Accessed on 24 January 2024)

[xxx] https://www.who.int/activities/amplifying-the-lived-experience-of-people-affected-by-cancer (Accessed on 24 January 2024)

[xxxi] https://www.frontier-economics.com/uk/en/news-and-articles/news/news-article-i20141-cost-of-preventable-cancers-in-the-uk-to-rise/ (Accessed on 14 January 2024)

xxxii https://www.crukcentre.manchester.ac.uk/engage/patient-public-involvement-and-engagement/#:~:text=Patient%20public%20involvement%20and%20engagement,or%20members%20of%20our%20community. (Accessed on 14 January 2024)

xxxiii https://www.hopkinsmedicine.org/research/understanding-clinical-trials/clinical-research-what-is-it#:~:text=Clinical%20research%20is%20different%20than,new%20ideas%20may%20help%20people (Accessed on 26 January 2024)

xxxiv https://www.forbes.com/sites/forbesbusinessdevelopmentcouncil/2023/07/13/the-importance-of-age-diversity-in-clinical-trials-and-proactive-steps-the-industry-can-take/?sh=3de2a76d420b (Accessed on 26 January 2024)

xxxv https://www.ncbi.nlm.nih.gov/pmc/articles/PMC4916819/ (Accessed on 26 January 2024)

xxxvi https://www.ncbi.nlm.nih.gov/pmc/articles/PMC2878987/#:~:text=All%20patients%20are%20recruited%20all,desired%20sample%20size%20is%20achieved (Accessed on 26 January 2024)

xxxvii https://www.ncbi.nlm.nih.gov/pmc/articles/PMC2878987/#b10-1530205 (Accessed on 26 January 2024)

xxxviii https://www.ncbi.nlm.nih.gov/pmc/articles/PMC1661624/ (Accessed on 26 January 2024)

xxxix https://acsjournals.onlinelibrary.wiley.com/doi/full/10.1002/cncr.32755 (Accessed on 26 January 2024)

xl https://www.ncbi.nlm.nih.gov/pmc/articles/PMC7342339/ (Accessed on 1 April 2024)

xli https://www.arraylive.com/blog/how-to-increase-clinical-trial-enrollment-with-information-and-communication#:~:text=In%20fact%2C%20nearly%2080%20percent,failure%20to%20a chieve%20full%20enrollment.&text=There%20are%20many%20reasons%20clinical,some%20key%20barriers%20to%20enrollment (Accessed on 26 January 2024)

xlii

https://journals.lww.com/cancernursingonline/abstract/2003/10000/challenges_of_recruitment_a_nd_retention_in.6.aspx (Accessed on 26 January 2024)

xliii https://journals.plos.org/plosone/article?id=10.1371/journal.pone.0127242 (Accessed on 26 January 2024)

xliv https://www.nhs.uk/conditions/clinical-trials/#:~:text=If%20you%20take%20part%20in%20a%20clinical%20trial%2C%20you%27ll,no%20proven%20standard%20treatment%20exists (Accessed on 26 January 2024)

xlv https://www.nihr.ac.uk/documents/briefing-notes-for-researchers-public-involvement-in-nhs-health-and-social-care-research/27371#democratic-principles (Accessed on 24 January 2024)

xlvi https://www.legislation.gov.uk/ukpga/2004/30/contents (Accessed on 24 January 2024)

xlvii https://www.who.int/teams/social-determinants-of-health/declaration-of-alma-ata (Accessed on 24 January 2024)

xlviii https://www.who.int/publications/i/item/WHO-HIS-SDS-2018.61 (Accessed on 26 January 2024)

xlix https://www.england.nhs.uk/wp-content/uploads/2017/04/ppp-policy-edit.pdf (Accessed on 26 January 2024)

l https://ascopubs.org/doi/10.1200/EDBK_100035 (Accessed on 26 January 2024)

li https://www.ncbi.nlm.nih.gov/pmc/articles/PMC6092479/ (Accessed on 26 January 2024)

lii https://sites.google.com/nihr.ac.uk/pi-standards/home (Accessed on 26 January 2024)

liii https://www.centerwatch.com/articles/25599-oncology-trials-outpacing-rest-of-the-field-in-complexity-and-duration-study-shows#:~:text=The%20number%20of%20investigational%20drugs,genetic%20sequencing%20technologies%2C%20CSDD%20says (Accessed on 26 January 2024)

liv https://www.cancer.net/research-and-advocacy/patient-advocates/being-cancer-advocate (Accessed on 26 January 2024)

lv https://cancer.ca/en/cancer-information/reduce-your-risk (Accessed on 26 January 2024)

lvi https://www.cancer.gov/publications/dictionaries/cancer-terms/ (Accessed on 28 April 2024)